The Tale of Two Kings:
An In-depth Study of The Covenants of God
Published by: Susan Moore

Copyright © 2017, TXu 2-080-927, by Susan Moore. All Rights reserved.

Reproduction of this text in whole or part without the express written consent of the author is not permitted and is unlawful according to The 1976 United States Copyright Act.

Unless otherwise indicated, all scriptural quotations are from the King James Version.

All rights reserved.

ISBN-13-9781724776891

ISBN-10-1724776894

Dedication

I dedicate this book to the love of my life and best friend, my husband Russ; to my wonderful children and grandchildren, who are the reason for staying in the faith and fighting the good fight; to my brother Mike and his wife Debbie for leading me to the Lord; and to my Mom, who is the reason for my being.

Acknowledgements

First and foremost, I would like to thank my heavenly Father for trusting me with this assignment. I thank Him for the many hours that He supped with me and opened the scriptures to me. I have truly been blessed by His goodness and mercy.

I would like to thank my Pastors, Winford and Catherine Ethridge, for giving me a love for studying and rightly dividing the word of truth.

I would like to thank my spiritual covering Apostle Lola Moore for all the prayers and encouragement.

I would like to thank all the men and women of God who have influenced my journey.

I want to thank my church family, Living Water Ministry, for the love and support that they have given me.

I want to thank Deliverance and Praise Chief Cornerstone Ministries' Pastor, Carrie Dunson, for always encouraging me to complete my assignment.

I want to thank Myra Bohannon for assisting me with the preparations of getting this book into print.

I thank all of you who read this study and I pray that you will be blessed by this gift that the Father has given to us, His children.

Comments

The Tale of Two Kings is an eye-opening offering of revolutionary insights into God's plan. How it is revealed through the scripture is beautifully direct.

- James Weaver

I really enjoyed the book. Sis. Moore is a very good teacher. It opened the scriptures up to me. Thank you, Sister Moore for allowing God to use you this way, giving you the knowledge to share to others. Thanks!

- Wanda Dunn

God in His infinite wisdom has opened this portion of His mysteries to Prophetess Susan Moore through The Holy Spirit.

When you complete this book, you will have a greater love and appreciation for the God that you serve or are seeking, as I did. This book of truth will reveal how intricate our Creator is. May God bless you continuously!

-Myra Bohannon

Forward

There is nothing more rewarding than to see the gift of knowledge working in someone's life and to witness the awakening of the scriptures.

This book has been a 3-year journey for my wife of dedicating herself to the mind of Christ through the obedience of the Spirit, as the opening of the scriptures would be given to her at all hours of the night and early in the morning. I would find her writing down the scriptures as God would reveal the Covenants to her as she studied the passages ("For flesh and blood has not revealed this, but the heavenly Father"–Matthew 16:17).

These Covenants reveal The LORD God in a way that I have never seen, and my wife will amaze you in this book that will bring revelation knowledge to you.

May her excitement come alive to you as it did to me as she was sharing each new revelation. May God bless you and open the scriptures to you.

- Pastor Russ Moore

Bibliography

The Holy Bible (King James Version)

 Table of Contents

Introduction

Chapter 1 - Tale of Two Kings...................... Page 15

Chapter 2 - Then the Spiritual .... Page 31

Chapter 3 - The Fall .... Page 65

Chapter 4 - The Covenant of Grace .... Page 81

Chapter 5 - The Covenant of Abraham .... Page 97

Chapter 6 - The Covenant of Law .... Page 109

Chapter 7 - The Covenant of Faith (The Final Covenant) . Page 121

Introduction

Tale of Two Kings

God has provided us the Holy Scriptures as a blueprint of His redemptive plan. From the first word penned in Genesis to the last word of Revelation we see a picture of His love. Each verse and chapter portraying grace and truth to all generations. When we search out these truths written in the books of the Bible we seek revelation knowledge through the Spirit of God.

> *2Timothy 3:16*
> *All scripture is given by inspiration of God, and is profitable for doctrine, for reproof, for correction, for instruction in righteousness:*

Moses wrote the book of Genesis having been born generations after the beginning. He sought God's glory and God revealed to him His goodness, His name, and His works from the foundation of the world. The book of Genesis is an account of this revelation.

> *Exodus 33:18 - 23*
> *18 - And he said, I beseech thee, shew me thy glory.*
> *19 - And he said, <u>I will make all my goodness pass before thee</u>, and <u>I will proclaim the name of the LORD before thee</u>; and will be gracious to whom I will be gracious, and will shew mercy on whom I will shew mercy.*
> *20 - And he said, Thou canst not see my face: for there shall no man see me, and live.*
> *21 - And the LORD said, Behold, there is a place by me, and thou shalt stand upon a rock:*
> *22 - And it shall come to pass, while my glory passeth by, that I will put thee in a clift of the rock, and will cover thee with my hand while I pass by:*
> *23 - And I will take away mine hand, <u>and thou shalt see my back parts:</u> but my face shall not be seen.*

> *Exodus 34:5 - 7*
> *5 - And the LORD descended in the cloud, and stood with him there, and proclaimed the name of the LORD.*
> *6 - And the LORD passed by before him, and proclaimed, <u>The LORD, The LORD God,</u> merciful and gracious, longsuffering, and abundant in goodness and truth,*
> *7 - Keeping mercy for thousands, forgiving iniquity and transgression and sin, and that will by no means clear the guilty; visiting the iniquity of the fathers upon the children, and upon the children's children, unto the third and to the fourth generation.*

> *Acts 15:18*
> *Known unto God are all his works from the beginning of the world.*

Solomon was wise above any other king and he wrote about God's omniscience. Through wisdom he understood that everything that had been or ever would be hung on God's word.

>*Ecclesiastes 3:14 - 15*
>*14 - I know that, whatsoever God doeth, it shall be for ever: nothing can be put to it, nor any thing taken from it: and God doeth it, that men should fear before him.*
>*15 - That which hath been is now; and that which is to be hath already been; and God requireth that which is past.*

We will start our study in the beginning.

>*Genesis 1:1 – 3*
>*1 - In the beginning God created the heaven and the earth.*
>*2 - And the earth was without form, and void; and darkness was upon the face of the deep. And the Spirit of God moved upon the face of the waters.*
>*3 - And God said, Let there be light: and there was light.*

>*John 1:1 – 2*
>*1 - In the beginning was the Word, and the Word was with God, and the Word was God.*
>*2 - The same was in the beginning with God.*

>*1John 1:1 – 2*
>*1 - That which was from the beginning, which we have heard, which we have seen with our eyes, which we have looked upon, and our hands have handled, of the Word of life;*
>*2 - (For the life was manifested, and we have seen it, and bear witness, and shew unto you that eternal life, which was with the Father, and was manifested unto us;)*

In the beginning God's spoken Word brought forth the Light and the Life. It is the very source of Life for man.

>*Matthew 4:4*
>*But he answered and said, It is written, Man shall not live by bread alone, but by every word that proceedeth out of the mouth of God.*

>*John 1:2 – 4*
>*2 - The same was in the beginning with God.*
>*3 - All things were made by him; and without him was not any thing made that was made.*
>*4 - In him was life; and the life was the light of men.*

God spoke Light into darkness and Life into nothingness. His Word of life came forth and brought life. When the Word came forth Light and Life came with it through the Spirit. Genesis through Malachi is an account of the written word. Matthew through Revelation is an account of the Living word.

> ***John 1:14***
> <u>***And the Word was made flesh***</u>***, and dwelt among us, (and we beheld his glory, the glory as of the only begotten of the Father,) full of grace and truth.***

Fulfilling God's plan from the beginning to put enmity between Satan and the woman, the seed of Satan and the seed of the woman.

> ***Genesis 3:15***
> ***And I will put enmity between thee and the woman, and between thy seed and her seed;*** <u>***it***</u> ***shall bruise thy head, and thou shalt bruise*** <u>***his***</u> ***heel.***

The <u>"it"</u> being the written word of God, and the <u>"his"</u> being the written word made flesh. The enmity brought forth by the promise of God in the garden. As we study the word of God he will unveil through revelation knowledge his divine purpose and pattern for our lives.

> ***John 10:10***
> ***The thief cometh not, but for to steal, and to kill, and to destroy: I am come that they might have life, and that they might have it more abundantly.***

The living Word gives life to all who seek after it. Abundant life is available to everyone who hungers and thirsts for truth. Every scripture revealing Jesus Christ beginning at Moses and the prophets and ending in Revelation.

> ***Luke 24:27***
> ***And beginning at Moses and all the prophets, he expounded unto them in all the scriptures the things concerning himself.***

> ***Revelation 1:8***
> ***I am Alpha and Omega, the beginning and the ending, saith the Lord, which is and which was, and which is to come****,* <u>***the Almighty.***</u>

> ***Revelation 19:13***
> ***And he was clothed with a vesture dipped in blood: and his name is called,*** <u>***The Word of God.***</u>

Through the scriptures we see Jesus from the beginning in Genesis to the ending in Revelation. The Word of God, the Light of the world and the Life of men.

> *John 1:1 – 4*
> *1 - In the beginning was the Word, and the Word was with God, and the Word was God.*
> *2 - The same was in the beginning with God.*
> *3 - All things were made by him; and without him was not any thing made that was made.*
> *4 - In him was life; and the life was the light of men.*
>
> *John 5:39*
> *Search the scriptures; for in them ye think ye have eternal life: and they are they which testify of me.*
>
> *John 6:48*
> *I am that bread of life.*
>
> *John 6:63*
> *It is the spirit that quickeneth; the flesh profiteth nothing: the words that I speak unto you, they are spirit, and they are life.*
>
> *Luke 4:4*
> *And Jesus answered him, saying, It is written, That man shall not live by bread alone, but by every word of God.*

Jesus is the Word of God. The door to the Kingdom of God.

> *John 10:9*
> *I am the door: by me if any man enter in, he shall be saved, and shall go in and out, and find pasture.*

He opened the scriptures;

> *Luke 24:27*
> *And beginning at Moses and all the prophets, he expounded unto them in all the scriptures the things concerning himself.*

He opened their eyes;

> *Luke 24:30 - 31*
> *30 - And it came to pass, as he sat at meat with them, he took bread, and blessed it, and brake, and gave to them.*
> *31 - And their eyes were opened, and they knew him; and he vanished out of their sight.*

He opened their understanding;

> *Luke 24:45*
> *Then opened he their understanding, that they might understand the scriptures,*

Through this study we will be seeking an entrance into his marvelous light.

> *2Corinthians 4:6*
> *For God, who commanded the light to shine out of darkness, hath shined in our hearts, to give the light of the knowledge of the glory of God in the face of Jesus Christ*

> *1Peter 2:9*
> *But ye are a chosen generation, a royal priesthood, an holy nation, a peculiar people; that ye should shew forth the praises of him who hath called you out of darkness into his marvellous light;*

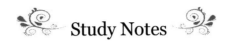

Chapter 1

Tale of Two Kings

When we search the Word of God we see patterns of heavenly things. Beginning in Genesis and carried through Revelation, we see the plan and purpose of a loving Heavenly Father bringing his children to the throne of grace. In this study we will be looking at types or patterns of the two covenants that the LORD God made with man. The first covenant with the house of Jacob and the second with the spiritual Israel. We read in the scripture that God separated the two.

> *Isaiah 43:1*
> *But now thus saith the LORD that created thee, O Jacob, and He that formed thee, O Israel, Fear not: for I have redeemed thee, I have called thee by thy name; thou art mine.*

In this prophecy we see that God stated that he first created Jacob then he formed Israel. He then redeemed him both naturally and spiritually. This is the order which we will be unfolding the mystery of the covenants, old and new.

> *Isaiah 43:18*
> *Remember ye not the former things, neither consider the things of old.*
>
> *Isaiah 43:19*
> *Behold, I will do a new thing; now it shall spring forth; shall ye not know it? I will even make a way in the wilderness, and rivers in the desert.*
>
> *Hebrews 8:13*
> *In that he saith, A new covenant, he hath made the first old. Now that which decayeth and waxeth old is ready to vanish away.*

We will search out the patterns of the heavenly tabernacle which is the true tabernacle.

> *Hebrews 8:1 – 2*
> *1 - Now of the things which we have spoken this is the sum: We have such an high priest, who is set on the right hand of the throne of the Majesty in the heavens;*
> *2 - A minister of the sanctuary, and of the true tabernacle, which the Lord pitched, and not man.*

The old would be replaced with a new and better covenant. An eternal covenant that would abide in the minds and the hearts of man. This eternal covenant would be made with Israel, not Jacob.

Hebrews 8:3 – 12
3 For every high priest is ordained to offer gifts and sacrifices: wherefore it is of necessity that this man have somewhat also to offer.
4 - For if he were on earth, he should not be a priest, seeing that there are priests that offer gifts according to the law:
5 - Who serve unto the example and shadow of heavenly things, as Moses was admonished of God when he was about to make the tabernacle: for, See, saith he, that thou make all things according to the pattern shewed to thee in the mount.
6 - But now hath he obtained a more excellent ministry, by how much also he is the mediator of a better covenant, which was established upon better promises.
7 - For if that first covenant had been faultless, then should no place have been sought for the second.
8 - For finding fault with them, he saith, Behold, the days come, saith the Lord, when I will make a new covenant with the house of Israel and with the house of Judah:
9 - Not according to the covenant that I made with their fathers in the day when I took them by the hand to lead them out of the land of Egypt; because they continued not in my covenant, and I regarded them not, saith the Lord.
10 - For this is the covenant that I will make with the house of Israel after those days, saith the Lord; I will put my laws into their mind, and write them in their hearts: and I will be to them a God, and they shall be to me a people:
11 - And they shall not teach every man his neighbour, and every man his brother, saying, Know the Lord: for all shall know me, from the least to the greatest.
12 - For I will be merciful to their unrighteousness, and their sins and their iniquities will I remember no more.

We will find out that everything in the old will be revealed and manifested in the new. Each type and shadow unveiled through the word itself. The works of God are eternal, revealing himself through time, past, present and future.

Ecclesiastes 3:14 - 15
14 - I know that, whatsoever God doeth, it shall be for ever: nothing can be put to it, nor any thing taken from it: and God doeth it, that men should fear before him.
15 - That which hath been is now; and that which is to be hath already been; and God requireth that which is past.

We will search out the natural and unlock the spiritual.

1Corinthians 15:46
Howbeit that was not first which is spiritual, but that which is natural; and afterward that which is spiritual.

We will study both the Old and the New Testament scriptures to come into the revelation knowledge of Jesus Christ.

> *Ephesians 1:17 - 18*
> *17 - That the God of our Lord Jesus Christ, the Father of glory, <u>may give unto you the spirit of wisdom and revelation in the knowledge of him</u>:*
> *18 - <u>The eyes of your understanding being enlightened</u>; that ye may know what is the hope of his calling, and what the riches of the glory of his inheritance in the saints,*

In this book we will be looking at two kings. One who was removed and one who was given an eternal covenant. Each one portraying one of the two types of Covenant of the Kingdom of God. The first whose kingdom was rent away from him and the one who it was given to. Paul himself expounded the gospel of Jesus using these two kings as a foundation of the work that God would bring forth. The revealing of the old into the new.

> *Acts 13:15 - 23*
> *15 - <u>And after the reading of the law and the prophets the rulers of the synagogue sent unto them, saying, Ye men and brethren, if ye have any word of exhortation for the people, say on.</u>*
> *16 - <u>Then Paul stood up</u>, and beckoning with his hand said, Men of Israel, and ye that fear God, give audience.*
> *17 - The God of this people of Israel chose our fathers, and exalted the people when they dwelt as strangers in the land of Egypt, and with an high arm brought he them out of it.*
> *18 - And about the time of forty years suffered he their manners in the wilderness.*
> *19 - And when he had destroyed seven nations in the land of Canaan, he divided their land to them by lot.*
> *20 - And after that he gave unto them judges about the space of four hundred and fifty years, <u>until Samuel the prophet.</u>*
> *21 - <u>And afterward they desired a king: and God gave unto them Saul the son of Cis, a man of the tribe of Benjamin, by the space of forty years.</u>*
> *22 - <u>And when he had removed him, he raised up unto them David to be their king; to whom also he gave testimony, and said, I have found David the son of Jesse, a man after mine own heart, which shall fulfil all my will.</u>*
> *23 - <u>Of this man's seed hath God according to his promise raised unto Israel a Saviour, Jesus:</u>*

> *1Samuel 13:8 – 10, 13 – 14*
> *8 - And he tarried seven days, according to the set time that Samuel had appointed: but Samuel came not to Gilgal; and the people were scattered from him.*
> *9 - <u>And Saul said, Bring hither a burnt offering to me, and peace offerings. And he offered the burnt offering.</u>*
> *10 - <u>And it came to pass, that as soon as he had made an end of offering the burnt offering, behold, Samuel came; and Saul went out to meet him, that he might salute him.</u>*

> *13 - <u>And Samuel said to Saul, Thou hast done foolishly: thou hast not kept the commandment of the LORD thy God, which he commanded thee: for now would the LORD have established thy kingdom upon Israel for ever.</u>*
> *14 - <u>But now thy kingdom shall not continue: the LORD hath sought him a man after his own heart, and the LORD hath commanded him to be captain over his people, because thou hast not kept that which the LORD commanded thee.</u>*

Because of Saul not keeping the commandment of the LORD another would be appointed to be king. David would be the key that would unlock the spiritual door to the Kingdom of God. God would build a tabernacle according to the one that David pitched.

> *2Samuel 6:12 – 19*
> *12 - And it was told King David, saying, The LORD hath blessed the house of Obededom, and all that pertaineth unto him, because of the ark of God. <u>So David went and brought up the ark of God from the house of Obededom into the city of David with gladness.</u>*
> *13 - And it was so, that when they that bare the ark of the LORD had gone six paces, <u>he sacrificed oxen and fatlings.</u>*
> *14 - <u>And David danced before the LORD with all his might; and David was girded with a linen ephod.</u>*
> *15 - So David and all the house of Israel brought up the ark of the LORD with shouting, and with the sound of the trumpet.*
> *16 - And as the ark of the LORD came into the city of David, Michal Saul's daughter looked through a window, and saw King David leaping and dancing before the LORD; and she despised him in her heart.*
> *17 - And they brought in the ark of the LORD, and set it in his place, in the midst of the tabernacle that David had pitched for it: <u>and David offered burnt offerings and peace offerings before the LORD.</u>*
> *18 - <u>And as soon as David had made an end of offering burnt offerings and peace offerings, he blessed the people in the name of the LORD of hosts.</u>*
> *19 - <u>And he dealt among all the people, even among the whole multitude of Israel, as well to the women as men, to every one a cake of bread, and a good piece of flesh, and a flagon of wine. So all the people departed every one to his house.</u>*
>
> *Acts 15:16 – 18*
> *16 - After this I will return, <u>and will build again the tabernacle of David, which is fallen down; and I will build again the ruins thereof, and I will set it up:</u>*
> *17 - That the residue of men might seek after the Lord, and all the Gentiles, upon whom my name is called, saith the Lord, who doeth all these things.*
> *18 - <u>Known unto God are all his works from the beginning of the world.</u>*

We see in this portion of scripture that David operated in both a kingly and priestly order. The kingdom of God was removed from Saul because he had given the sacrifice himself instead of waiting on Samuel. Through this study we will understand why this was such a significant event. To be able to understand why the LORD made a difference between Saul and David we will search out the word of God. We will start this study from the beginning in the book of Genesis. It is an account of God's goodness, name and works. It was written by Moses after God had revealed his glory. In Genesis we can find revelation of God's redemption.

> *Exodus 33:18 - 23*
> *18 - And he said, I beseech thee, shew me thy glory.*
> *19 - And he said, I will make all my goodness pass before thee, and I will proclaim the name of the LORD before thee; and will be gracious to whom I will be gracious, and will shew mercy on whom I will shew mercy.*
> *20 - And he said, Thou canst not see my face: for there shall no man see me, and live.*
> *21 - And the LORD said, Behold, there is a place by me, and thou shalt stand upon a rock:*
> *22 - And it shall come to pass, while my glory passeth by, that I will put thee in a clift of the rock, and will cover thee with my hand while I pass by:*
> *23 - And I will take away mine hand, <u>and thou shalt see my back parts: but my face shall not be seen.</u>*
>
> *Exodus 34:5 - 7*
> *5 - <u>And the LORD descended in the cloud, and stood with him there, and proclaimed the name of the LORD.</u>*
> *6 - And the LORD passed by before him, and proclaimed, <u>The LORD, The LORD God, merciful and gracious, longsuffering, and abundant in goodness and truth,</u>*
> *7 - <u>Keeping mercy for thousands, forgiving iniquity and transgression and sin, and that will by no means clear the guilty; visiting the iniquity of the fathers upon the children, and upon the children's children, unto the third and to the fourth generation.</u>*

We see in verse 23 that he was going to show Moses his back parts, the things that had already been and would be. He would reveal his future by his past. He would stand upon a rock and would be hidden in the rock with God's hand upon him, but he would not know the significance of it. He would proclaim the name of the LORD to him, but he would not have the glory of the name. Moses would know the beginning but not the ending. He would partake of the natural but not the spiritual. This confirms the scriptures that we have read.

> *Ecclesiastes 3:14 – 15*
> *14 - I know that, <u>whatsoever God doeth, it shall be for ever: nothing can be put to it, nor any thing taken from it: and God doeth it,</u> that men should fear before him.*
> *15 - <u>That which hath been is now; and that which is to be hath already been; and God requireth that which is past.</u>*
>
> *Acts 15:18*
> <u>*Known unto God are all his works from the beginning of the world.*</u>

First, The Natural

> *1Corinthians 15:46a*
> *Howbeit that was not first which is spiritual, but that which is natural;*

<u>The Word, The Light and The Life</u>

> *Genesis 1:1*
> *In the beginning God created <u>the heaven and the earth.</u>*

We understand by this scripture that this will be an account of God creating. Notice that the subject is <u>the heaven and the earth.</u> The heaven being singular. As we study you will see the significance of this point.

> *Genesis 1:2*
> *And the earth was without form, and void; and darkness was upon the face of the deep. And the Spirit of God moved upon the face of the waters.*

When we look at this verse there are three things that we observe:

- The earth had no form and was void.
- Darkness was already present.
- The Spirit of God moved.

> *Genesis 1:3*
> *And God said, Let there be light: and there was light.*

The first thing that God did was speak and His word brought light. This was not the creation of the sun and the moon and the stars but a creative force. The earth was without form and void and darkness was upon the face of the deep. We understand that darkness is the absence of light. God was about to bring form to the earth by speaking Himself into it. The voice of God brought forth light and this light was the creative life. He separated light from darkness therefore establishing two realms of existence. These two would always be separate never to coexist. God is light and in him is no darkness at all. Life could only exist in the light brought forth by his word.

> *John 1:1 – 2*
> *1 - In the beginning was <u>the Word, and the Word was with God, and the Word was God.</u>*
> *2 - The same was in the beginning with God.*

> *1John 1:5*
> *This then is the message which we have heard of him, and declare unto you, that <u>God is light, and in him is no darkness at all.</u>*

> *John 1:3 – 4*
> *3 - All things were made by him; and without him was not any thing made that was made.*
> *4 - In him was <u>life</u>; and the <u>life</u> was the <u>light</u> of men.*

The three things that were brought:
- The Word
- The Light
- The Life

These three things moved with God's Spirit to form and create. He made a separation between the light and the darkness. He called the light day and the darkness night, this was the first day. God always starts out by separating light and darkness. He separated it when he created the heaven and the earth, and he separated it when he entered the heaven and the earth. He will separate it when he returns to it. This separation between light and darkness, Day and Night will be the very essence of man's search for truth. Our study begins and ends with the same. There are many scriptures that confirm this truth. We will look at a few. My prayer is that you will take time to search them out and pray for Jesus to open your understanding.

> *Genesis 1:4 – 5*
> *4 - And God saw the light, that it was good: and God divided the light from the darkness.*
> *5 - And God called the light Day, and the darkness he called Night. And the evening and the morning were the first day.*

<u>Word</u>

> *John 1:1*
> *In the beginning was <u>the Word</u>, and <u>the Word was with God</u>, and <u>the Word was God.</u>*
>
> *John 1:14*
> *And <u>the Word</u> was made flesh, and dwelt among us, (and we beheld His glory, the glory as of the only begotten of the Father) full of grace and truth.*
>
> *1John 1:1 - 2*
> *1 - That which was from the beginning, which we have heard, which we have seen with our eyes, which we have looked upon, and our hands have handled, of <u>the Word of life</u>;*
> *2 - (For the life was manifested, and we have seen it, and bear witness, and shew unto you that eternal life, which was with the Father, and was manifested unto us;)*

1John 5:7
For there are three that bear record in heaven, the Father<u>, the Word</u>, and the Holy Ghost: and these three are one.

Revelation 19:13
And he was clothed with a vesture dipped in blood: and his name is called <u>The Word of God.</u>

Light

Genesis 1:3
And God said, Let there be <u>light:</u> and there was <u>light.</u>

John 1:5 - 13
5 - And the <u>light</u> shineth in darkness; and the darkness comprehended it not.
6 - There was a man sent from God, whose name was John.
7 - The same came for a witness, to bear witness of the <u>Light</u>, that all men through him might believe.
8 - He was not that <u>Light</u>, but was sent to bear witness of that <u>Light.</u>
9 - That was the true <u>Light,</u> which lighteth every man that cometh into the world.
10 - He was in the world, and the world was made by him, and the world knew him not.
11 - He came unto his own, and his own received him not.
12 - But as many as received him, to them gave He power to become the sons of God, even to them that believe on His name:
13 - Which were born, not of blood, nor of the will of the flesh, nor of the will of man, but of God.

John 12:46
I am come a <u>light</u> into the world, that whosoever believeth on me should not abide in darkness.

John 3:19 - 21
19 - And this is the condemnation, that <u>light</u> is come into the world, and men loved darkness rather than <u>light</u>, because their deeds were evil.
20 - For every one that doeth evil hateth the <u>light</u>, neither cometh to the <u>light</u>, lest his deeds should be reproved.
21 - But he that doeth truth cometh to the <u>light</u>, that his deeds may be made manifest, that they are wrought in God.

1Thessalonians 5:5
Ye are all the children of <u>light</u>, and the children of the day: we are not of the night, nor of darkness.

<u>Life</u>

Proverbs 8:35
<u>*For whoso findeth me findeth life*</u>, *and shall obtain favour of the LORD.*

John 3:16
For God so loved the world, that he gave his only begotten Son, that whosoever believeth in him should not perish, but have everlasting <u>life.</u>

John 3:36
He that believeth on the Son hath everlasting <u>life</u>: and he that believeth not the Son shall not see <u>life;</u> but the wrath of God abideth on him.

John 5:26
For as the Father hath <u>life</u> in himself; so hath he given to the Son to have <u>life</u> in himself;

John 5:39
Search the scriptures; for in them ye think ye have eternal <u>life</u>: and they are they which testify of me.

John 5:40
And ye will not come to me, that ye might have <u>life.</u>

John 6:33
For the bread of God is he which cometh down from heaven, and giveth life unto the world.

John 6:47 - 48
47 - Verily, verily, I say unto you, He that believeth on me hath everlasting <u>life.</u>
48 - I am that bread of life.

John 14:6
Jesus saith unto him, I am the way, the truth, and the <u>life</u>: no man cometh unto the Father, but by me.

Acts 3:13 - 15
13 - The God of Abraham, and of Isaac, and of Jacob, the God of our fathers, hath glorified his Son Jesus; whom ye delivered up, and denied him in the presence of Pilate, when he was determined to let him go.
14 - But ye denied the Holy One and the Just, and desired a murderer to be granted unto you;
15 - And killed the <u>Prince of life</u>, whom God hath raised from the dead; whereof we are witnesses.

We see Jesus woven throughout the scriptures. The word of God made flesh, from the beginning to the end. God's plan to redeem fallen man. The way (light), the truth (word), and the life (Prince of life). Everlasting life.

> ***John 8:58***
> ***Jesus said unto them, Verily, verily, I say unto you, Before Abraham was, I am.***
>
> ***Hebrews 13:8***
> ***Jesus Christ the same yesterday, and to day, and for ever.***
>
> ***Revelation 1:10***
> ***I was in the Spirit on the Lord's day, and heard behind me <u>a great voice</u>, as of a trumpet,***
>
> ***Revelation 1:11***
> ***Saying, I am Alpha and Omega, the first and the last:***
>
> ***Revelation 1:17 - 18***
> ***17 - And when I saw him, I fell at his feet as dead. And he laid his right hand upon me, saying unto me, Fear not; I am the first and the last:***
> ***18 - <u>I am He that liveth</u>, and <u>was dead</u>; and, behold, <u>I am alive for evermore</u>, Amen; <u>and have the keys of hell and of death.</u>***

"He that liveth" - We must take note here that He said, "I am He that liveth". The word liveth is a continuation. He did not say lived, which denotes past tense but rather a continual life. He used past tense when He referred to death. He was speaking of the flesh that was crucified, not of the Spirit that was from the beginning.

"I am alive for evermore" is referring to the risen state of the man Christ Jesus.

"And have the keys of hell and death" - We can see by the order of this that these are spiritual keys. Hell comes after natural death and life comes after resurrection from death. Many times, people misquote this by saying He has the keys to death, hell and the grave.

The scripture says that it is appointed to men to die therefore he does not have the keys to the grave. **(Hebrews 9:27 - And as it is appointed unto men once to die, but after this the judgment).** Thus, this clarifies the order of hell and death. As mediator between God and man He is the door between time and eternity and has the keys to unlock eternal life.

> ***1Timothy 2:5***
> ***For there is one God, and one mediator between God and men, the man Christ Jesus;***
>
> ***Hebrews 9:15***
> ***And for this cause he is the mediator of the New Testament, that by means of death, for the redemption of the transgressions that were under the first testament, they which are called might receive the promise of eternal inheritance.***

Hebrews 12:24
And to Jesus the mediator of the new covenant, and to the blood of sprinkling, that speaketh better things than that of Abel.

We understand by the scriptures that Moses was a mediator of the law, the Old Testament. The shadow of the better covenant which was a promise to **the seed** which was Christ. The law was given because of transgressions. When we look at King Saul we see that God granted them a king because of their rejection of him. He was then replaced by King David because he did not keep the commandments.

1Samuel 8:4 - 9
4 - Then all the elders of Israel gathered themselves together, and came to Samuel unto Ramah,
5 - And said unto him, Behold, thou art old, and thy sons walk not in thy ways: now make us a king to judge us like all the nations.
6 - But the thing displeased Samuel, when they said, Give us a king to judge us. And Samuel prayed unto the LORD.
7 - And the LORD said unto Samuel, Hearken unto the voice of the people in all that they say unto thee: for they have not rejected thee, but they have rejected me, that I should not reign over them.
8 - According to all the works which they have done since the day that I brought them up out of Egypt even unto this day, wherewith they have forsaken me, and served other gods, so do they also unto thee.
9 - Now therefore hearken unto their voice: howbeit yet protest solemnly unto them, and shew them the manner of the king that shall reign over them.

Acts 13:21 - 22
21 - And afterward they desired a king: and God gave unto them Saul the son of Cis, a man of the tribe of Benjamin, by the space of forty years.
22 - And when he had removed him, he raised up unto them David to be their king; to whom also he gave testimony, and said, I have found David the son of Jesse, a man after mine own heart, which shall fulfil all my will.

Galatians 3:19
Wherefore then serveth the law? It was added because of transgressions, till the seed should come to whom the promise was made; and it was ordained by angels in the hand of a mediator.

Galatians 3:16
Now to Abraham and his seed were the promises made. He saith not, And to seeds, as of many; but as of one, And to thy seed, which is Christ.

The Heaven and The Earth

> ***Isaiah 43:1***
> ***But now thus saith the LORD that created thee, O Jacob***

We will look first at the natural, the creation of the heaven and the earth and the natural man. God does everything in order and we will see this pattern of the natural first, then the spiritual throughout this study.

> ***Genesis 1:1***
> ***In the beginning God <u>created</u> <u>the heaven and the earth.</u>***
>
> ***1Corinthians 15:46***
> ***<u>Howbeit that was not first which is spiritual, but that which is natural; and afterward that which is spiritual.</u>***

We understand by the scriptures that the Old Testament was types and shadows of what was to come. A pattern of heavenly things that would be replaced with better things. He referred to the tabernacle of Moses as a covenant by stating that there would be a better covenant.

> ***Hebrews 8:5 - 6***
> ***5 - Who serve unto the example and shadow of heavenly things, as Moses was admonished of God when he was about to make <u>the tabernacle</u>: for, See, saith he, that thou make all things according to the pattern shewed to thee in the mount.***
> ***6 - But now hath he obtained a more excellent ministry, by how much also he is the mediator of a <u>better covenant</u>, which was established upon <u>better promises</u>.***
>
> ***Hebrews 9:23-24***
> ***23 - <u>It was therefore necessary that the patterns of things in the heavens should be purified with these; but the heavenly things themselves with better sacrifices than these.</u>***
> ***24 - <u>For Christ is not entered into the holy places made with hands, which are the figures of the true; but into heaven itself, now to appear in the presence of God for us:</u>***

With this pattern in mind we will look at the creation of The Heaven and The Earth.

> ***Genesis 1:4 - 5***
> ***4 - And God saw the light, that it was good: and God divided the light from the darkness.***
> ***5 - And God called the light Day, and the darkness he called Night. And the evening and the morning were the first day.***

After God had separated light and darkness, Day and Night, he then began the creation of the Heaven and the Earth. Everything that followed the first day would be created in light (Day). He began creation with Himself. God is always first when pertaining to life.

> *Genesis 1:6 - 8*
> *6 - And God said, Let there be a firmament in the midst of the waters, and let it divide the waters from the waters.*
> *7 - And God made the firmament, and divided the waters which were under the firmament from the waters which were above the firmament: and it was so.*
> *8 - And God called the firmament Heaven. And the evening and the morning were the second day.*

The earth was covered with water in the beginning. God divided the waters and set the natural Heaven into place. He then began to bring form to the Earth. Light would bring form to the earth, in darkness there was no form.

> *Genesis 1:9 – 10*
> *9 - And God said, Let the waters under the heaven be gathered together unto one place, and let the dry land appear: and it was so.*
> *10 - And God called the dry land Earth; and the gathering together of the waters called He Seas: and God saw that it was good.*

The dry land was now Earth, the firmament above was Heaven and the water was called Seas. God set forth the boundaries and the laws of nature. Everything from this moment forward would be subject to those laws.

> *Genesis 1:11 – 12*
> *11 - And God said, <u>Let the earth bring forth grass, the herb yielding seed, and the fruit tree yielding fruit after his kind, whose seed is in itself, upon the earth: and it was so.</u>*
> *12 - <u>And the earth brought forth grass, and herb yielding <u>seed</u> after his kind, and the tree yielding fruit, whose <u>seed</u> was in itself, after his kind:</u> and God saw that it was good.*

The first law of the earth was the law of seed. The earth was called to bring forth for as long as it would exist. God set it in place in the beginning and he does not have to reseed the earth afterwards. It is a law of nature for the earth to renew itself. Therefore, when God flooded the earth in the days of Noah that the earth was able to renew itself. It renews itself after a plowing or a fire or a flood. It is a law that doesn't have to be reinstated every time there is a purging of the earth. Left alone the earth will be able to renew itself.

> *Genesis 1:14 – 19*
> *14 - And God said, Let there be lights in the firmament of the heaven to divide the day from the night; and let them be for signs, and <u>for seasons, and for days, and years:</u>*

15 - And let them be for lights in the firmament of the heaven to give light upon the earth: and it was so.
16 - And God made two great lights; the greater light to rule the day, and the lesser light to rule the night: he made the stars also.
17 - And God set them in the firmament of the heaven to give light upon the earth,
18 - And to rule over the day and over the night, and to divide the light from the darkness: and God saw that it was good.
19 - And the evening and the morning were the fourth day.

The next law that God would set would be for signs and seasons, days and years, the Law of Time. Seedtime and harvest would be continuous as long as the sun, the moon and the stars remain in the Heaven. Time would continue for all generations past, present and future.

Ecclesiastes 3:1 - 8
1 - To every thing there is a <u>season, and a time</u> to every purpose under <u>the heaven:</u>
2 - A time to be born, and a time to die; a time to plant, and a time to pluck up that which is planted;
3 - A time to kill, and a time to heal; a time to break down, and a time to build up;
4 - A time to weep, and a time to laugh; a time to mourn, and a time to dance;
5 - A time to cast away stones, and a time to gather stones together; a time to embrace, and a time to refrain from embracing;
6 - A time to get, and a time to lose; a time to keep, and a time to cast away;
7 - A time to rend, and a time to sew; a time to keep silence, and a time to speak;
8 - A time to love, and a time to hate; a time of war, and a time of peace.

From this point on all that God would create would be subject to time. Every creature would have a time to be born and a time to die, all plant life would have a season.

Genesis 1:20 – 23
20 - And God said<u>, Let the waters bring forth abundantly the moving creature that hath life, and fowl that may fly above the earth in the open firmament of heaven.</u>
21 - And God created great whales, and every living creature that moveth<u>, which the waters brought forth abundantly,</u> after their kind, and every winged fowl after his kind: and God saw that it was good.
22 - And God blessed them, saying, Be fruitful, and multiply, and fill the waters in the seas, and let fowl multiply in the earth.
23 - And the evening and the morning were the fifth day.

The next law that God would set would be the law of Life. God placed DNA into the waters with his word. Life would be a continuation in the Seas and the Natural Heaven. He commanded the waters to bring forth and blessed what it brought. The Seas continue to bring forth life today. The discovery of new life is continual.

Genesis 1:24 – 28
24 - And God said, <u>Let the earth bring forth the living creature after his kind, cattle, and creeping thing, and beast of the earth after his kind: and it was so.</u>
25 - And God made the beast of the earth after his kind, and cattle after their kind, and every thing that creepeth upon the earth after his kind: and God saw that it was good.
26 - <u>And God said, Let us make man in our image, after our likeness: and let them have dominion over the fish of the sea, and over the fowl of the air, and over the cattle, and over all the earth, and over every creeping thing that creepeth upon the earth.</u>
27 - So God created man in his own image, in the image of God created he him; male and female created he them.
28 - And God blessed them, and God said unto them, Be fruitful, and multiply, and replenish the earth, and subdue it: and have dominion over the fish of the sea, and over the fowl of the air, and over every living thing that moveth upon the earth.

God commanded the Earth to bring forth Life. God set DNA into the earth with His Word. The law of Species was set in place by God. This would do away with any preconceived notion that man could come from an animal. Each species would bring forth after his kind, this does not do away with adaptation. Each living thing was created with the ability to adapt to the climate or area in which it was brought forth. This is evident in nature itself, because that it was not created in a mold, but it was brought forth by the Earth. We see a difference in the physical aspects of the creation according to the environment where they live but not the species. A dog will always give birth to a dog, a cat to a cat, a horse to a horse, etc. The law of nature was set in order by God and blessed in the beginning.

God created man in his image. He did not command that the waters bring forth man, nor the earth bring him forth. He would create man in his very essence. He would give man, his image in his DNA. We began this study by looking at what was brought forth before the creation began. The Word, The Light and The Life - these three things would be the image of the natural man. He would have the capacity for language, the ability to bring forth thoughts and ideas to reason and plan for creative ability, and for reproducing life. He would have dominion over the natural Heaven and Earth. He would be able to utilize the laws that God had set in order to prosper his life in the Earth. He was given the position to rule over every living thing in the sea, the heaven and the earth.

Genesis 1:29 – 31
29 - And God said, Behold, I have given you every herb bearing seed, which is upon the face of all the earth, and every tree, in the which is the fruit of a tree yielding seed; to you it shall be for meat.
30 - And to every beast of the earth, and to every fowl of the air, and to every thing that creepeth upon the earth, wherein there is life, I have given every green herb for meat: and it was so.
31 - And God saw every thing that he had made, and, behold, it was very good. And the evening and the morning were the sixth day.

God then set the order of provision for the life of the natural man and all living things. He provided to His creation a continual source of food. I would like to point out at this time that God gave all the herbs and fruits of all the trees in the earth to man. This completed the creation of the natural heaven and the earth. The dominion of man was set in <u>the heaven and the earth.</u> The natural was complete.

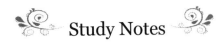

Chapter 2

Then the Spiritual

FINISHED

>*Genesis 2:1*
>*<u>Thus the heavens and the earth were finished</u>, and all the host of them.*

We read in Genesis chapter one the account of the creation of the natural <u>heaven and earth.</u> Chapter two begins by saying that the <u>heavens</u> and the earth were finished with all the host of them. This denotes that there existed <u>heavens</u> before the natural <u>heaven</u> was created along with <u>the host</u> of heaven. The word finished states a completion of God's creation. Leading us to understand that the creation account of the heaven and the earth in chapter one was the final creation of God.

>*Nehemiah 9:6*
>*Thou, even thou, art LORD alone; thou hast made <u>heaven</u>, the <u>heaven of heavens</u>, with all their host, <u>the earth, and all things that are therein, the seas, and all that is therein</u>, and thou preservest them all; and <u>the host of heaven worshippeth thee.</u>*

>*Isaiah 45:12*
>*I have made <u>the earth</u>, and created man upon it: I, even my hands, have stretched out <u>the heavens</u>, and all their host have I commanded.*

>*Isaiah 45:18*
>*For thus saith the LORD that created <u>the heavens</u>; God himself that formed <u>the earth</u> and made it; he hath established it, he created it not in vain, He formed it to be inhabited: I am the LORD; and there is none else.*

>*Isaiah 48:13*
>*Mine hand also hath laid the foundation of <u>the earth</u>, and my right hand hath spanned <u>the heavens</u>: when I call unto them, they stand up together.*

These scriptures state the heavens to be plural and the earth singular. The scriptures say that God created the natural heaven and earth in six days, but heavens already existed.

>*Exodus 20:11*
>*For <u>in six days</u> the LORD made <u>heaven and earth, the sea, and all that in them is,</u> and rested the seventh day: wherefore the LORD blessed the sabbath day, and hallowed it.*

>*Exodus 31:17*
>*It is a sign between me and the children of Israel for ever: for <u>in six days</u> the LORD made <u>heaven and earth</u>, and on the seventh day he rested, and was refreshed.*

This denotes that the natural heaven and earth were created in time but the heavens that already existed were not. The spiritual heavens are the dwelling of God therefore, they are eternal for God is eternal. They are spiritual for God is a Spirit. They are not set in time but in eternity.

> *John 4:24*
> *God is a Spirit: and they that worship him must worship him in spirit and in truth.*
>
> *Romans 1:20*
> *For the invisible things of him from the creation of the world are clearly seen, being understood by the things that are made, even his eternal power and Godhead; so that they are without excuse:*
>
> *2Corinthians 4:18*
> *While we look not at the things which are seen, but at the things which are not seen: for the things which are seen are temporal; but the things which are not seen are eternal.*
>
> *1Timothy 1:17*
> *Now unto the King eternal, immortal, invisible, the only wise God, be honour and glory for ever and ever. Amen.*

REST

> *Genesis 2:2 – 3*
> *2 - And on the seventh day God ended his work which he had made; and he rested on the seventh day from all his work which he had made.*
> *3 - And God blessed the seventh day, and sanctified it: because that in it he had rested from all his work which God created and made.*

The word finished denotes a time of completion. When he finished his work, God set aside a time of rest. He blessed it and sanctified it and he established it as a time of refreshing. He also set a day of Sabbath for man as a day of rest and refreshing. The seventh day rest was instituted into the law as a figure of the rest and refreshing that he would send after he finished the work of redemption of fallen man. We also want to remember that Jesus spoke of another day when referring to the rest as recorded in Hebrews 4:8-9. He set man's time of work equivalent to his -six days. The seventh day being signified as a day of rest.

> *1Chronicles 23:25*
> *For David said, The LORD God of Israel hath given rest unto his people, that they may dwell in Jerusalem for ever:*

When looking at David we read that the LORD God had given an eternal rest to Israel in Jerusalem. This rest pertained to the covenant that God made with David. This would not be a natural rest but a spiritual rest. The natural is subject to time but the spiritual is not. God is a spirit. The seventh day rest was a spiritual rest.

Exodus 23:12
<u>Six days</u> thou shalt do thy work, and on the seventh day <u>thou shalt rest</u>: that thine ox and thine ass may rest, and the son of thy handmaid, and the stranger, <u>may be refreshed.</u>

This rest was a natural rest because it was set in time, a pattern of what would come. This rest followed natural labor, first the natural then the spiritual. This rest was established under the law of commandments.

Isaiah 28:11 – 12
11 - <u>For with stammering lips and another tongue will he speak to this people.</u>
12 - To whom he said, <u>This is the rest wherewith ye may cause the weary to rest</u>; <u>and this is the refreshing: yet they would not hear.</u>

Isaiah 32:17 – 18
17 - And the work of righteousness shall be peace; and the effect of righteousness quietness and assurance for ever.
18 - And my people shall dwell in a peaceable habitation, and in sure dwellings, and <u>in quiet resting places;</u>

Hebrews 4:1 – 11
1 - <u>Let us therefore fear, lest, a promise being left us of entering into his rest, any of you should seem to come short of it.</u>
2 - <u>For unto us was the gospel preached, as well as unto them: but the word preached did not profit them, not being mixed with faith in them that heard it.</u>
3 - <u>For we which have believed do enter into rest,</u> as he said, As I have sworn in my wrath, if they shall enter into my rest: <u>although the works were finished from the foundation of the world.</u>
4 - For he spake in a certain place of the seventh day on this wise, <u>And God did rest the seventh day from all his works.</u>
5 - And in this place again, <u>If they shall enter into my rest.</u>
6 - Seeing therefore it remaineth that some must enter therein, <u>and they to whom it was first preached entered not in because of unbelief:</u>
7 - <u>Again, he limiteth a certain day</u>, saying in David, To day, after so long a time; as it is said, To day if ye will hear his voice, harden not your hearts.
8 - <u>For if Jesus had given them rest, then would he not afterward have spoken of another day.</u>
9 - <u>There remaineth therefore a rest to the people of God.</u>
10 -<u>For he that is entered into his rest</u>, he also hath ceased from his own works, as God did from his.
11 - <u>Let us labour therefore to enter into that rest, lest any man fall after the same example of unbelief.</u>

These scriptures refer to a spiritual rest, an eternal rest. This rest would also follow labor but it would not be natural labor. This rest was established in the new covenant. It is a rest for the spiritual man, not the natural.

LABOUR

Proverbs 10:16
The labour of the righteous tendeth to life: the fruit of the wicked to sin.

Matthew 3:8
Bring forth therefore fruits meet for repentance:

Luke 3:8
Bring forth therefore fruits worthy of repentance, and begin not to say Within yourselves, We have Abraham to our father: for I say unto you, That God is able of these stones to raise up children unto Abraham.

John 6:27
Labour not for the meat which perisheth, but for that meat which endureth unto everlasting life, which the Son of man shall give unto you: for him hath God the Father sealed.

Acts 26:20
But shewed first unto them of Damascus, and at Jerusalem, and throughout all the coasts of Judaea, and then to the Gentiles, that they should repent and turn to God, and do works meet for repentance.

Acts 3:19
Repent ye therefore, and be converted, that your sins may be blotted out, when the times of refreshing shall come from the presence of the Lord;

In these verses we read that spiritual rest followed repentance. On the day of Pentecost an entrance was opened for that rest.

Acts 2:1 – 4
1 - And when the day of Pentecost was fully come, they were all with one accord in one place.
2 - And suddenly there came a sound from heaven as of a rushing mighty wind, and it filled all the house where they were sitting.
3 - And there appeared unto them cloven tongues like as of fire, and it sat upon each of them.
4 - And they were all filled with the Holy Ghost, and began to speak with other tongues, as the Spirit gave them utterance.

We read that Hebrews 4: 7-8 speaks of a certain day. The day of Pentecost was fully come when God poured out his Spirit upon all flesh as prophesied in Joel 2:28-29.

Joel 2:28 – 29
28 - And it shall come to pass afterward, that I will pour out my spirit upon all flesh; and your sons and your daughters shall prophesy, your old men shall dream dreams, your young men shall see visions:
29 - And also upon the servants and upon the handmaids in those days will I pour out my spirit.

> *Acts 2:14 - 18*
> *14 - But Peter, standing up with the eleven, lifted up his voice, and said unto them, Ye men of Judaea, and all ye that dwell at Jerusalem, be this known unto you, and hearken to my words:*
> *15 - For these are not drunken, as ye suppose, seeing it is but the third hour of the day.*
> *16 - <u>But this is that which was spoken by the prophet Joel;</u>*
> *17 - <u>And it shall come to pass in the last days, saith God, I will pour out of my Spirit upon all flesh: and your sons and your daughters shall prophesy, and your young men shall see visions, and your old men shall dream dreams:</u>*
> *18 - <u>And on my servants and on my handmaidens I will pour out in those days of my Spirit; and they shall prophesy:</u>*

Isaiah prophesied of the rest and the refreshing that they would not hear. The words, they would not hear, tells us that it would be a sound.

> *Isaiah 28:11 – 12*
> *11 - <u>For with stammering lips and another tongue will he speak to this people.</u>*
> *12 - <u>To whom he said, This is the rest wherewith ye may cause the weary to rest; and this is the refreshing: yet they would not hear.</u>*

Peter also spoke of the pouring out of the Holy Ghost on the day of Pentecost.

> *Acts 2:25 – 28, 31 – 39*
> *25 - For David speaketh concerning him, I foresaw the Lord always before my face, for he is on my right hand, that I should not be moved:*
> *26 - Therefore did my heart rejoice, and my tongue was glad; moreover also my flesh shall rest in hope:*
> *27 - <u>Because thou wilt not leave my soul in hell</u>, neither wilt thou suffer thine Holy One to see corruption.*
> *28 - Thou hast made known to me the ways of life; thou shalt make me full of joy with thy countenance.*
>
> *31 - He seeing this before spake of the resurrection of Christ, that his soul was not left in hell, neither his flesh did see corruption.*
> *32 - <u>This Jesus hath God raised up, whereof we all are witnesses.</u>*
> *33 - <u>Therefore being by the right hand of God exalted, and having received of the Father the promise of the Holy Ghost, he hath shed forth this, which ye now see and hear.</u>*
> *34 - For David is not ascended into the heavens: but he saith himself, The LORD said unto my Lord, Sit thou on my right hand,*
> *35 - Until I make thy foes thy footstool.*
> *36 - Therefore let all the house of Israel know assuredly, that God hath made that same <u>Jesus, whom ye have crucified, both Lord and Christ.</u>*
> *37 - <u>Now when they heard this,</u> they were pricked in their heart, and said unto Peter and to the rest of the apostles, Men and brethren, what shall we do?*

> **38 - Then Peter said unto them, Repent, and be baptized every one of you in the name of Jesus Christ for the remission of sins, and ye shall receive the gift of the Holy Ghost.**
> **39 - For the promise is unto you, and to your children, and to all that are afar off, even as many as the Lord our God shall call.**

These scriptures reveal to us that entering the rest that God had promised could only be accomplished by faith. The labor that would be required was works of repentance and doing the will of the Father. This rest was a refreshing for the people of God, a promise for all who would be called.

> *Matthew 11:28 - 30*
> *28 - Come unto me, <u>all ye that labour and are heavy laden</u>, and I will give you <u>rest</u>.*
> *29 - Take my yoke upon you, and learn of me; for I am meek and lowly in heart: and ye shall find <u>rest</u> unto your souls.*
> *30 - For my yoke is easy, and <u>my burden is light</u>.*

We need to remember that Hebrews said that we labor to enter the spiritual rest and scripture said that our labor is works of repentance. With this we can know that Jesus is addressing those who repent and are under the burden of sin. The burden that he will give to replace sin is light. Light is life and we can only find rest in the light of God. The promise is a place of rest.

> *John 14:1 – 3*
> *1 - Let not your heart be troubled: ye believe in God, believe also in me.*
> *2 - In my Father's house are many mansions: if it were not so, I would have told you. <u>I go to prepare a place for you.</u>*
> *3 - <u>And if I go and prepare a place for you, I will come again, and receive you unto myself; that where I am, there ye may be also.</u>*

Jesus stated that he was going to prepare a place. Hebrews 4:10 revealed that Jesus has entered into his rest.

> *Hebrews 4:10*
> *<u>For he that is entered into his rest</u>, he also hath ceased from his own works, as God did from his.*

This clarifies the statement that Jesus made in Matthew 11:28-30

> *Matthew 11:28 – 30*
> *28 - Come unto me, <u>all ye that labour and are heavy laden</u>, and I will give you <u>rest</u>.*
> *29 - Take my yoke upon you, and learn of me; for I am meek and lowly in heart: and ye shall find <u>rest</u> unto your souls.*
> *30 - For my yoke is easy, and <u>my burden is light</u>.*

We can only find rest in the risen savior Christ Jesus. He has prepared a place for us that where he is, we are also. He has prepared for us a spiritual resting place.

A SIGN OF SANCTIFICATION

> *Exodus 31:13*
> *Speak thou also unto the children of Israel, saying, Verily my Sabbaths ye shall keep: for it is a sign between me and you throughout your generations; that ye may know that <u>I am the LORD that doth sanctify you.</u>*

> *Ezekiel 20:12*
> *Moreover also I gave them my Sabbaths, to be a sign between me and them, that they might know that <u>I am the LORD that sanctify them.</u>*

In these verses we read that the rest is sanctification.

PERPETUAL COVENANT

> *Exodus 31:16*
> *Wherefore the children of Israel shall keep the Sabbath, to observe the Sabbath throughout their generations, <u>for a perpetual covenant.</u>*

It is a perpetual covenant, an eternal one. We remember that the tabernacle of Moses would be replaced with a better covenant. The better one would be a perpetual one.

THE SUMMARY

To sum this section up we will go to Isaiah.

> *Isaiah 30:15*
> *For thus saith the Lord GOD, the Holy One of Israel; <u>In returning and rest shall ye be saved</u>; in quietness and in confidence shall be your strength: <u>and ye would not.</u>*

> *Isaiah 28:11 – 12*
> *11 - <u>For with stammering lips and another tongue will he speak to this people.</u>*
> *12 - <u>To whom he said, This is the rest wherewith ye may cause the weary to rest; and this is the refreshing: yet they would not hear.</u>*

This seventh day rest is a spiritual rest not a natural. Repentance is the way to enter this rest. The Holy Ghost is the rest and the refreshing. Under the old covenant they would not hear, repent and be saved.

THE NATURAL AND THE SPIRITUAL

Genesis 2:4
These are the generations of the heavens and of the earth when they were created, in the <u>day that the LORD God made the earth and the heavens,</u>

This scripture reveals to us that the following will be both a natural (earth) and a spiritual (heavens) account of the creation of Adam. We must take notice that it states LORD God, not just God as it did in chapter one. We read that in Genesis 1:1 that God created the <u>heaven</u> and <u>the earth</u> with heaven being singular. This shows that when pertaining to the natural realm He is God, yet pertaining to both the natural and the spiritual realm He is LORD God, Covenant God. We will study the following account with this concept in mind.

1Corinthians 2:14
<u>But the natural man receiveth not the things of the Spirit of God: for they are foolishness unto him: neither can he know them, because they are spiritually discerned.</u>

1Corinthians 15:44
It is sown a natural body; it is raised a spiritual body. <u>There is a natural body, and there is a spiritual body.</u>

1Corinthians 15:46
<u>Howbeit that was not first which is spiritual, but that which is natural; and afterward that which is spiritual.</u>

The word makes a definite distinction between the natural and the spiritual. Paul wrote that the natural was first, then the spiritual. This scripture coincides with the account of creation in Genesis.

VISIBLE AND INVISIBLE

Romans 1:20
For <u>the invisible things of him from the creation of the world are clearly seen, being understood by the things that are made, even his eternal power and Godhead; so that they are without excuse:</u>

Colossians 1:16
<u>For by him were all things created, that are in heaven, and that are in earth, visible and invisible, whether they be thrones, or dominions, or principalities, or powers: all things were created by him, and for him:</u>

Hebrews 11:3
Through faith we understand that <u>the worlds were framed by the word of God, so that things which are seen were not made of things which do appear.</u>

These scriptures reveal that there are two realms of life. The natural which is visible and the spiritual which is invisible. The natural realm will always be subject to time, the spiritual will not for it is eternal. When Paul was speaking to the Corinthians referring to the resurrection of man he stated the order of creation. He, being a scholar of the word, understood that man was first natural then spiritual. Man was first corruptible then incorruptible, mortal then immortal. The natural man could not discern the things of the Spirit.

BOTH NATURAL AND SPIRITUAL (VISIBLE AND INVISIBLE)

> *Isaiah 43:1*
> *But now thus saith the LORD that created thee, O Jacob, and He that formed thee, O Israel,*

This scripture denotes that Jacob was the natural that was created and that Israel which represented the spiritual was formed. We will use this pattern to look at Adam.

> *Genesis 2:7 – 8*
> *7 - And the LORD God formed man of the dust of the ground, and breathed into his nostrils the breath of life; and man became a living soul.*
> *8 - And the LORD God planted a garden eastward in Eden; and there he put the man whom he had formed.*

The man whom God formed was of the dust of the ground, the Earth first.

> *Romans 5:14*
> *Nevertheless death reigned from Adam to Moses, even over them that had not sinned after the similitude of Adam's transgression, who is the figure of him that was to come.*

> *John 14:3*
> *And if I go and prepare a place for you, I will come again, and receive you unto myself; that where I am, there ye may be also.*

We see that the LORD God formed man of the dust and then placed the man that he formed into the garden of Eden. That man was a figure of him who was to come. That man was both natural and spiritual. Jesus was both natural and spiritual as Adam was. He existed in both realms at the same time.

NATURAL

> *Isaiah 43:1*
> <u>*But now thus saith the LORD that created thee, O Jacob*</u>

> *Genesis 1:27 – 28*
> *27 -* <u>*So God created man in his own image, in the image of God created he him; male and female created he them.*</u>
> *28 - And God blessed them, and God said unto them,* <u>*Be fruitful, and multiply, and replenish the earth, and subdue it: and have dominion over the fish of the sea, and over the fowl of the air, and over every living thing that moveth upon the earth.*</u>

Some doctrines teach that man was created spirit because he was created in the image of God. Scripture states that the earth was created, and spirit was given. God did not create spirit, he gave it because he is spirit. God created natural man and gave natural man, dominion over the natural earth.

> *Ecclesiastes 12:7*
> *Then shall the dust return to the earth as it was:* <u>*and the spirit shall return unto God who gave it.*</u>

NATURAL FIRST, THEN SPIRITUAL

These verses confirm that the natural would be placed into the spiritual. It makes comparison to David who was natural and Jesus who was both natural and spiritual as Adam was. The covenant that the LORD God made with David was for a seed that would sit on the throne of Israel forever. David could not because he was a natural man.

> *Isaiah 43:1(b)*
> *...* <u>*and he that formed thee, O Israel,*</u>

> *Genesis 2:7 – 8*
> *7 -* <u>*And the LORD God formed man of the dust of the ground, and breathed into his nostrils the breath of life; and*</u> <u>*man became a living soul.*</u>
> *8 - And the LORD God planted a garden* <u>*eastward in Eden*</u>*; and there* <u>*he put the man whom he had formed.*</u>

> *Romans 5:14*
> *Nevertheless death reigned from Adam to Moses, even over them that had not sinned after the similitude of Adam's transgression, who is the* <u>*figure of him that was to come.*</u>

> *John 14:3*
> <u>*And if I go and prepare a place for you, I will come again, and receive you unto myself; that where I am, there ye may be also.*</u>

Romans 9:6 - 8
6 - Not as though the word of God hath taken none effect. <u>For they are not all Israel, which are of Israel:</u>
7 - Neither, because they are the seed of Abraham, are they all children: but, In Isaac shall thy seed be called.
8 - <u>That is, They which are the children of the flesh, these are not the children of God: but the children of the promise are counted for the seed.</u>

Acts 2:31 -36
31 - He seeing this before spake of the resurrection of Christ, that his soul was not left in hell, neither his flesh did see corruption.
32 - <u>This Jesus hath God raised up, whereof we all are witnesses.</u>
33 - <u>Therefore being by the right hand of God exalted, and having received of the Father the promise of the Holy Ghost, he hath shed forth this, which ye now see and hear.</u>
34 - <u>For David is not ascended into the heavens: but he saith himself, The LORD said unto my Lord, Sit thou on my right hand,</u>
35 - Until I make thy foes thy footstool.
36 - Therefore let all the house of Israel know assuredly<u>, that God hath made that same Jesus, whom ye have crucified, both Lord and Christ.</u>

1Corinthians 15:42 – 49
42 - <u>So also is the resurrection of the dead. It is sown in corruption; it is raised in incorruption:</u>
43 - <u>It is sown in dishonour; it is raised in glory: it is sown in weakness; it is raised in power:</u>
44 - <u>It is sown a natural body; it is raised a spiritual body. There is a natural body, and there is a spiritual body.</u>
45 - <u>And so it is written, The first man Adam was made a living soul; the last Adam was made a quickening spirit.</u>
46 - <u>Howbeit that was not first which is spiritual, but that which is natural; and afterward that which is spiritual.</u>
47 - <u>The first man is of the earth, earthy: the second man is the Lord from heaven.</u>
48 - <u>As is the earthy, such are they also that are earthy: and as is the heavenly, such are they also that are heavenly.</u>
49 - <u>And as we have borne the image of the earthy, we shall also bear the image of the heavenly.</u>

1Corinthians 15:53 -54
53 - <u>For this corruptible must put on incorruption, and this mortal must put on immortality.</u>
54 - <u>So when this corruptible shall have put on incorruption, and this mortal shall have put on immortality, then shall be brought to pass the saying that is written, Death is swallowed up in victory.</u>

We read in the account of the creation of the natural heaven and earth that God had created everything that was created to be under the law of seasons, days and years. Paul was explaining the mystery of eternal life to men who had always been subject to time. God created man earthly first; he was formed of the dust of the earth and the earth was subject to seasons, days and years. The earth and all the creation of the earth was subject to time. In order to form dust, it must first be mixed with water. The Spirit of God is referred to as water. The breath of God is referred to as life. The LORD God mixed time with eternity. The LORD God mixed earth and heavens and <u>man became a living soul.</u>

> *Genesis 2:7*
> <u>*And the LORD God formed man of the dust of the ground, and breathed into his nostrils the breath of life; and man became a living soul.*</u>

Man became a living soul when God formed him and breathed into him the breath of life. We can conclude then that life comes through the water of life and the breath of God.

> *John 4:14*
> <u>*But whosoever drinketh of the water that I shall give him shall never thirst; but the water that I shall give him shall be in him a well of water springing up into everlasting life.*</u>

> *John 7:37 – 39*
> *37 - In the last day, that great day of the feast, Jesus stood and cried, saying, <u>If any man thirst, let him come unto me, and drink.</u>*
> *38 - He that believeth on me, as the scripture hath said, <u>out of his belly shall flow rivers of living water.</u>*
> *39 - <u>(But this spake he of the Spirit, which they that believe on him should receive: for the Holy Ghost was not yet given; because that Jesus was not yet glorified.)</u>*

> *John 20:22*
> *And when he had said this<u>, he breathed on them, and saith unto them, Receive ye the Holy Ghost:</u>*

> *Revelation 21:6*
> *And he said unto me, It is done. I am Alpha and Omega, the beginning and the end. <u>I will give unto him that is athirst of the fountain of the water of life freely</u>.*

> *Revelation 22:1*
> <u>*And he shewed me a pure river of water of life*</u>*, clear as crystal, proceeding out of the throne of God and of the Lamb.*

> *Revelation 22:17*
> *And the Spirit and the bride say, Come. And let him that heareth say, Come. And let him that is athirst come. And whosoever will, let him take the water of life freely.*

EARTHLY AND HEAVENLY IMAGE

> *1Corinthians 15:47 – 49*
> *47 - <u>The first man is of the earth, earthy</u>: the second man is the Lord from heaven.*
> *48 - <u>As is the earthy, such are they also that are earthy</u>: and as is the heavenly, such are they also that are heavenly.*
> *49 - <u>And as we have borne the image of the earthy</u>, we shall also bear the image of the heavenly.*

We understand that Paul is speaking past tense when he says that we <u>have borne the image of the earthly.</u> The phrase "<u>we shall</u>" speaks of future tense. This scripture speaks of another day just like Hebrews 4:8-11. The rest would come after the time of labor has ceased. Romans 5:14 reveals that Adam was the figure of him that was to come. A figure is a type, pattern or resemblance of the true. 1 Corinthians 15, The first man Adam was made a living soul. The last Adam was made a quickening spirit. Jesus himself separated the natural and the spiritual when talking to Nicodemus.

> *John 3:5 – 8*
> *5 - Jesus answered, Verily, verily, I say unto thee, <u>Except a man be born of water and of the Spirit,</u> he cannot enter into the kingdom of God.*
> *6 - <u>That which is born of the flesh is flesh; and that which is born of the Spirit is spirit.</u>*
> *7 - Marvel not that I said unto thee, <u>Ye must be born again.</u>*
> *8 - <u>The wind bloweth where it listeth, and thou hearest the sound thereof, but canst not tell whence it cometh, and whither it goeth: so is every one that is born of the Spirit.</u>*

Jesus is declaring that those that are born of the Spirit would become part of the invisible realm, a realm where only the effects can be seen. This same concept can be seen in the garden of Eden. We read that God first formed man of the dust of the earth (mortal), then breathed into him the breath of life (immortality). He then planted a garden and he placed the man in the garden (spiritual). He then made to grow the tree of life and the tree of knowledge of good and evil. He formed Adam in his rest on the seventh day. He placed him into the invisible, the spiritual.

> *Genesis 2:1 – 4, 7 - 9*
> *1 - Thus the heavens and the earth were finished, and all the host of them.*
> *2 - And on the seventh day God ended his work which he had made; and he rested on the seventh day from all his work which he had made.*
> *3 - And God blessed the seventh day, and sanctified it: because that in it he had rested from all his work which God created and made.*
> *4 - These are the generations of the <u>heavens</u> and of the <u>earth</u> when they were created, <u>in the day that the LORD God made the earth and the heavens,</u>*
>
> *7 - <u>And the LORD God formed man of the dust of the ground, and breathed into his nostrils the breath of life; and man became a living soul.</u>*
> *8 - And the LORD God planted a garden <u>eastward in Eden; and there he put the man whom he had formed.</u>*

> *9 - And out of the ground made the LORD God to grow every tree that is pleasant to the sight, and good for food; the tree of life also in the midst of the garden, <u>and the tree of knowledge of good and evil.</u>*

In the creation of the natural heaven and earth God had the earth to bring forth the trees before he created man. In the spiritual heaven God planted a garden and placed the man, in it before he grew the trees. This signifies that this will be a work that God will do after he forms man. He gave man all the trees for food in the earth. In the garden he commanded the man not to eat of <u>the tree of THE knowledge of good and evil. In verse 9 it reads "the tree of knowledge of good and evil". In verse 17 it reads "the tree of THE knowledge of good and evil". By this we can know that the fruit of the tree is **THE knowledge**</u> of good and evil. God was commanding Adam not to eat **THE knowledge of good and evil.**

> *Genesis 2:15 – 17*
> *15 - And the LORD God took the man, and put him into the garden of Eden to dress it and to keep it.*
> *16 - And the LORD God commanded the man, saying, Of every tree of the garden thou mayest freely eat:*
> *17 - But of <u>the tree of the knowledge of good and evil</u>, thou shalt not eat of it: for in the day that thou eatest thereof thou shalt surely die.*

This indicates that the Garden of Eden was not a natural place but a spiritual. Man was not created in the Garden of Eden but placed there. He was to dress it, signifies that the man was to sow and to reap in the garden (the spirit). Paul referred to this in Galatians. He was to keep it, signifies that Adam would have to keep something to remain in the garden.

> *Galatians 6:8*
> *For he that soweth to his flesh shall of the flesh reap corruption; <u>but he that soweth to the Spirit shall of the Spirit reap life everlasting.</u>*

> *Isaiah 56:6*
> *Also the sons of the stranger, that join themselves to the LORD, to serve him, and to love the name of the LORD, to be his servants, every one <u>that keepeth the Sabbath from polluting it, and taketh hold of my covenant;</u>*

> *Revelation 3:8*
> *I know thy works: behold, I have set before thee an open door, and no man can shut it: for thou hast a little strength, <u>and hast kept my word</u>, and hast not denied my name.*

We understand by the scriptures that Jesus, (after he ceased from his work) entered the heavenly place in the same order as the account of Adam being put into the garden. First natural - then spiritual, Adam was a figure (type or shadow) of Him who was to come.

Genesis 2:7 - 8
<u>7 - And the LORD God formed man of the dust of the ground, and breathed into his nostrils the breath of life; and man became a living soul.</u>
<u>8 - And the LORD God planted a garden eastward in Eden; and there he put the man whom he had formed.</u>

Romans 5:14
Nevertheless death reigned from Adam to Moses, <u>even over them that had not sinned after the similitude of Adam's transgression,</u> who is the <u>figure of him</u> that was to come.

We must take note here that man became a living soul. When God told Adam not to eat of the tree of the knowledge of good and evil he said that the effect of it would be death. Scripture refers to the natural man as dead, the result of Adam's transgression. This death was a spiritual death.

Matthew 8:22
But Jesus said unto him, Follow me; and let the dead bury their dead.

Matthew 22:32
I am the God of Abraham, and the God of Isaac, and the God of Jacob? God is not the God of the dead, but of the living.

Mark 12:27
He is not the God of the dead, but the God of the living: ye therefore do greatly err.

Luke 9:60
Jesus said unto him, Let the dead bury their dead: but go thou and preach the kingdom of God.

Luke 20:38
For he is not a God of the dead, but of the living: for all live unto him.

John 5:21
For as the Father raiseth up the dead, and quickeneth them; even so the Son quickeneth whom he will.

John 5:25
Verily, verily, I say unto you, The hour is coming, and now is, when the dead shall hear the voice of the Son of God: and they that hear shall live.

John 11:25
Jesus said unto her, I am the resurrection, and the life: he that believeth in me, though he were dead, yet shall he live:

Romans 5:15
But not as the offence, so also is the free gift. For if through the offence of one many be dead, much more the grace of God, and the gift by grace, which is by one man, Jesus Christ, hath abounded unto many.

1Corinthians 15:21
For since by man came death, by man came also the resurrection of the dead.

2Corinthians 5:14
For the love of Christ constraineth us; because we thus judge, that if one died for all, then were all dead:

Ephesians 2:1
And you hath he quickened, who were dead in trespasses and sins;

Ephesians 2:5
Even when we were dead in sins, hath quickened us together with Christ, (by grace ye are saved;)

Ephesians 5:14
Wherefore he saith, Awake thou that sleepest, and arise from the dead, and Christ shall give thee light.

Colossians 1:18
And he is the head of the body, the church: who is the beginning, the firstborn from the dead; that in all things he might have the preeminence.

Colossians 2:13
And you, being dead in your sins and the uncircumcision of your flesh, hath he quickened together with him, having forgiven you all trespasses;

1Timothy 5:6
But she that liveth in pleasure is dead while she liveth.

By these scriptures we know that life only exists in the Spirit. Jesus came to give us life both in the natural and in the heavens.

Psalm 110:1
A Psalm of David. The LORD said unto my Lord, <u>Sit thou at my right hand, until I make thine enemies thy footstool.</u>

Isaiah 48:13
Mine hand also hath laid the foundation of the earth, and <u>my right hand hath spanned the heavens</u>: when I call unto them, they stand up together.

John 14:2-3
2-In my Father's house are many mansions: if it were not so, I would have told you. I go to prepare a place for you.
3-And if I go and prepare a place for you, I will come again, and receive you unto myself; that where I am, there ye may be also.

John 20:17
Jesus saith unto her, Touch me not; for I am not yet ascended to my Father: but go to my brethren, and say unto them, I ascend unto my Father, and your Father; and to my God, and your God.

Hebrews 4:8 – 11
8 - For if Jesus had given them rest, then would he not afterward have spoken of another day.
9 - There remaineth therefore a rest to the people of God.
10 - For he that is entered into his rest, he also hath ceased from his own works, as God did from his.
11 - Let us labour therefore to enter into that rest, lest any man fall after the same example of unbelief.

1Corinthians 15:42 - 49
42 - So also is the resurrection of the dead. It is sown in corruption; it is raised in incorruption:
43 - It is sown in dishonour; it is raised in glory: it is sown in weakness; it is raised in power:
44 - It is sown a natural body; it is raised a spiritual body. There is a natural body, and there is a spiritual body.
45 - And so it is written, The first man Adam was made a living soul; the last Adam was made a quickening spirit.
46 - Howbeit that was not first which is spiritual, but that which is natural; and afterward that which is spiritual.
47 - The first man is of the earth, earthy: the second man is the Lord from heaven.
48 - As is the earthy, such are they also that are earthy: and as is the heavenly, such are they also that are heavenly.
49 - And as we have borne the image of the earthy, we shall also bear the image of the heavenly.

We have a promise that when we cease from our work, we will enter into that rest that was prepared from the foundation of the world, where God has now placed us in the Spirit but will place us in our bodies.

HEAVENLY PLACES

The scripture states heavenly places (plural).

> *Luke 23:43*
> *And Jesus said unto him, Verily I say unto thee, To day shalt thou be with me in paradise.*
>
> *Ephesians 1:3*
> *Blessed be the God and Father of our Lord Jesus Christ, who hath blessed us with all spiritual blessings in heavenly places in Christ:*
>
> *Ephesians 1:20*
> *Which he wrought in Christ, when he raised him from the dead, and set him at his own right hand in the heavenly places,*
>
> *Ephesians 2:6*
> *And hath raised us up together, and made us sit together in heavenly places in Christ Jesus:*
>
> *Hebrews 4:3*
> *For we which have believed do enter into rest, as he said, As I have sworn in my wrath, if they shall enter into my rest: although the works were finished from the foundation of the world.*
>
> *Revelation 2:7*
> *He that hath an ear, let him hear what the Spirit saith unto the churches; To him that overcometh will I give to eat of the tree of life, which is in the midst of the paradise of God.*
>
> *John 14:2-3*
> *2-In my Father's house are many mansions: if it were not so, I would have told you. I go to prepare a place for you.*
> *3-And if I go and prepare a place for you, I will come again, and receive you unto myself; that where I am, there ye may be also.*

When Jesus made this statement to the disciples he was still present with them, yet He said "where I am, there ye may be also." He was still in the flesh, yet he spoke of being in a place that the disciples were not. A place that he would have to prepare for them. When God put Adam in the garden he made to grow the tree of life and the tree of knowledge of good and evil. The garden was a spiritual place, a place of knowledge.

> *John 12:23 - 28*
> *23 - And Jesus answered them, saying, The hour is come, that the Son of man should be glorified.*
> *24 - Verily, verily, I say unto you, Except a corn of wheat fall into the ground and die, it abideth alone: but if it die, it bringeth forth much fruit.*
> *25 - He that loveth his life shall lose it; and he that hateth his life in this world shall keep it unto life eternal.*

26 - <u>If any man serve me, let him follow me; and where I am, there shall also my servant be:</u> if any man serve me, him will my Father honour.
27 - Now is my soul troubled; and what shall I say? Father, save me from this hour: but for this cause came I unto this hour.
28 - Father, glorify thy name. Then came there a voice from heaven, saying, I have both glorified it, and will glorify it again.

John 17:24 – 25
24 - Father, I will that they also, whom thou hast given me<u>, be with me where I am;</u> that they may behold my glory, which thou hast given me: for thou lovedst me before the foundation of the world.
25 - O righteous Father, <u>the world hath not known thee: but I have known thee, and these have known that thou hast sent me.</u>

These scriptures reveal to us that the first heavenly place that Jesus mentioned was a place of knowledge. The second heavenly place would be where the Son of man would be glorified at the right hand of God.

Matthew 25:32 – 34
32 - And before him shall be gathered all nations: and he shall separate them one from another, as a shepherd divideth his sheep from the goats:
33 - <u>And he shall set the sheep on his right hand</u>, but the goats on the left.
34 - Then shall the King say unto them on his right hand, Come, ye blessed of my Father, <u>inherit the kingdom prepared for you from the foundation of the world:</u>

Mark 14:62
And Jesus said, I am: and ye shall see the Son of man sitting on the right hand of power, and coming in the clouds of heaven.

Acts 2:32 – 35
32- -<u>This Jesus hath God raised up,</u> whereof we all are witnesses.
33 - <u>Therefore being by the right hand of God exalted</u>, and having received of the Father the promise of the Holy Ghost, he hath shed forth this, which ye now see and hear.
34 - For David is not ascended into the heavens: but he saith himself, <u>The LORD said unto my Lord, Sit thou on my right hand,</u>
35 - Until I make thy foes thy footstool.

John 20:17
Jesus saith unto her, Touch me not; for I am not yet ascended to my Father: but go to my brethren, and say unto them, <u>I ascend unto my Father, and your Father; and to my God, and your God.</u>

Psalms 110:1
A Psalm of David. The LORD said unto my Lord<u>, Sit thou at my right hand, until I make thine enemies thy footstool.</u>

Isaiah 48:13
Mine hand also hath laid the foundation of the earth, and <u>my right hand hath spanned the heavens</u>: when I call unto them, they stand up together.

This is an eternal place, a place in the heavens. Peter said that God raised Jesus up, referring to the natural man, the Son of man. We studied earlier that the heavens were eternal because they are the dwelling place of God and God is eternal. The second heavenly place would be an eternal place for resurrected man (Son of man, flesh), in His kingdom. The following are scriptures that reveal the two places.

A PLACE OF KNOWLEDGE

Jeremiah 24:7
And I will give them an heart <u>to know me</u>, that I am the LORD: and they shall be my people, and I will be their God: for they shall return unto me with their whole heart.

John 17:3
<u>*And this is life eternal, that they might know thee the only true God, and Jesus Christ, whom thou hast sent.*</u>

Luke 1:76 – 79
76 - And thou, child, shalt be called the prophet of the Highest: for thou shalt go before the face of the Lord to prepare his ways;
77 - <u>To give knowledge of salvation unto his people by the remission of their sins,</u>
78 - Through the tender mercy of our God; whereby the dayspring from on high hath visited us,
79 - To give light to them that sit in darkness and in the shadow of death, to guide our feet into the way of peace.

2Corinthians 4:6
For God, who commanded the light to shine out of darkness, hath shined in our hearts, <u>to give the light of the knowledge of the glory of God in the face of Jesus Christ.</u>

Ephesians 4:13
Till we all come in the unity of the faith, <u>and of the knowledge of the Son of God, unto a perfect man, unto the measure of the stature of the fulness of Christ:</u>

2Peter 1:1 -3
1 - Simon Peter, a servant and an apostle of Jesus Christ, to them that have obtained like precious faith with us through the righteousness of God and our Saviour Jesus Christ:
2 - Grace and peace be multiplied unto you through the knowledge of God, and of Jesus our <u>Lord,</u>
3 - <u>According as his divine power hath given unto us all things that pertain unto life and godliness, through the knowledge of him that hath called us to glory and virtue:</u>

2Peter 1:8
<u>*For if these things be in you, and abound, they make you that ye shall neither be barren nor unfruitful in the knowledge of our Lord Jesus Christ.*</u>

2Peter 2:20
For if after they have escaped the pollutions of the world through the knowledge of the Lord and Saviour Jesus Christ, they are again entangled therein, and overcome, the latter end is worse with them than the beginning.

2Peter 3:18
But grow in grace, and in the knowledge of our Lord and Saviour Jesus Christ. To him be glory both now and for ever. Amen.

Ephesians 1:17
That the God of our Lord Jesus Christ, the Father of glory, may give unto you the spirit of wisdom and revelation in the knowledge of him:

THE KINGDOM

Isaiah 48:13
Mine hand also hath laid the foundation of the earth, and my right hand hath spanned the heavens: when I call unto them, they stand up together.

Matthew 25:32 – 34
32 - And before him shall be gathered all nations: and he shall separate them one from another, as a shepherd divideth his sheep from the goats:
33 - And he shall set the sheep on his right hand, but the goats on the left.
34 - Then shall the King say unto them on his right hand, Come, ye blessed of my Father, inherit the kingdom prepared for you from the foundation of the world:

Luke 12:32
Fear not, little flock; for it is your Father's good pleasure to give you the kingdom.

Luke 22:29 – 30
29 - And I appoint unto you a kingdom, as my Father hath appointed unto me;
30 - That ye may eat and drink at my table in my kingdom, and sit on thrones judging the twelve tribes of Israel.

Luke 23:42 – 43
42 - And he said unto Jesus, Lord, remember me when thou comest into thy kingdom.
43 - And Jesus said unto him, Verily I say unto thee, To day shalt thou be with me in paradise.

Acts 2:32 – 35
32 - This Jesus hath God raised up, whereof we all are witnesses.
33 - Therefore being by the right hand of God exalted, and having received of the Father the promise of the Holy Ghost, he hath shed forth this, which ye now see and hear.

34 - For David is not ascended into the heavens: but he saith himself, <u>The LORD said unto my Lord, Sit thou on my right hand,</u>
35 - Until I make thy foes thy footstool.

1Corinthians 15:42 – 49
42 - So also is the resurrection of the dead. It is sown in corruption; it is raised in incorruption:
43 - It is sown in dishonour; it is raised in glory: it is sown in weakness; it is raised in power:
44 - It is sown a natural body; it is raised a spiritual body. There is a natural body, and there is a spiritual body.
45 - And so it is written, <u>The first man Adam was made a living soul; the last Adam was made a quickening spirit.</u>
46 - <u>Howbeit that was not first which is spiritual, but that which is natural; and afterward that which is spiritual.</u>
47 - <u>The first man is of the earth, earthy: the second man is the Lord from heaven.</u>
48 - <u>As is the earthy, such are they also that are earthy: and as is the heavenly, such are they also that are heavenly.</u>
49 - <u>And as we have borne the image of the earthy, we shall also bear the image of the heavenly.</u>

Revelation 2:7
He that hath an ear, let him hear what the Spirit saith unto the churches; To him that overcometh <u>will I give to eat of the tree of life, which is in the midst of the paradise of God.</u>

There are many other scriptures that confirm these truths of the heavenly places in Christ Jesus. I pray that you will search out these scriptures for yourself. Paul wrote to Timothy to study to show himself approved unto God.

2Timothy 2:15
Study to shew thyself approved unto God, a workman that needeth not to be ashamed, rightly dividing the word of truth.

THE GARDEN

> *Genesis 2:8 – 15*
> *8 - And the LORD God planted a garden eastward in Eden; and there he put the man whom he had formed.*
> *9 - And out of the ground made the LORD God to grow every tree that is pleasant to the sight, and good for food; the tree of life also in the midst of the garden, and the tree of knowledge of good and evil.*
> *10 - And a river went out of Eden to water the garden; and from thence it was parted, and became into four heads.*
> *11 - The name of the first is Pison: that is it which compasseth the whole land of Havilah, where there is gold;*
> *12 - And the gold of that land is good: there is bdellium and the onyx stone.*
> *13 - And the name of the second river is Gihon: the same is it that compasseth the whole land of Ethiopia.*
> *14 - And the name of the third river is Hiddekel: that is it which goeth toward the east of Assyria. And the fourth river is Euphrates.*
> *15 - <u>And the LORD God took the man, and put him into the garden of Eden to dress it and to keep it.</u>*

We have understood that LORD God refers to covenant God. God planted the garden eastward in Eden and placed the man whom he had formed there. Paul stated that Adam was a figure of Him who was to come. We can know then that when God planted the garden that he did so with Christ in mind. The tree of life grew in the midst of the garden and the tree of knowledge of good and evil. We will search out truth with these points in mind.

Along with the tree of life and the tree of knowledge of good and evil, there was a river. The river went out of Eden to water the garden. The river parted into four heads from the garden. Each head of the river went to four different directions until all the land was covered. To understand the garden, we must go to the scriptures and search out The LORD God or covenant God. We find a man named Abram with whom the LORD made covenant.

> *Genesis 12:1 – 3*
> *1 - Now the LORD had said unto Abram, Get thee out of thy country, and from thy kindred, and from thy father's house, unto a land that I will shew thee:*
> *2 - And I will make of thee a great nation, and I will bless thee, and make thy*
> *name great; and thou shalt be a blessing:*
> *3 - And I will bless them that bless thee, and curse him that curseth thee: and in thee shall all families of the earth be blessed.*

> *Genesis 15:18*
> *In the same day <u>the LORD made a covenant with Abram, saying, Unto thy seed have I given this land, from the river of Egypt unto the great river, the river Euphrates:</u>*

Genesis 17:1 -8
1 - And when Abram was ninety years old and nine, <u>the LORD appeared to Abram</u>, and said unto him, <u>I am the Almighty God</u>; walk before me, and be thou perfect.
2 - And I will make my covenant between me and thee, and will multiply thee exceedingly.
3 - And Abram fell on his face: and God talked with him, saying,
4 - As for me, behold, my covenant is with thee, and thou shalt be a father of many nations.
5 - Neither shall thy name any more be called Abram, but thy name shall be Abraham; for a father of many nations have I made thee.
6 - And I will make thee exceeding fruitful, and I will make nations of thee, and kings shall come out of thee.
7 - <u>And I will establish my covenant between me and thee and thy seed after thee in their generations for an everlasting covenant, to be a God unto thee, and to thy seed after thee.</u>
8 - <u>And I will give unto thee, and to thy seed after thee, the land wherein thou art a stranger, all the land of Canaan, for an everlasting possession; and I will be their God.</u>

Genesis 22:16 – 18
16 - And said, By myself have I sworn, saith the LORD, for because thou hast done this thing, and hast not withheld thy son, thine only son:
17 - That in blessing I will bless thee, and in multiplying I will multiply thy seed as the stars of the heaven, and as the sand which is upon the sea shore; and thy seed shall possess the gate of his enemies;
18 - And in thy seed shall all the nations of the earth be blessed; because thou hast obeyed my voice.

Through these scriptures we see that the LORD made covenant with a man named Abram that would cover all the earth. This covenant would be an everlasting covenant with his seed. The LORD said by himself he hath sworn it.

Genesis 28:1 – 4; 10 – 14
1 - And Isaac called Jacob, and blessed him, and charged him, and said unto him, Thou shalt not take a wife of the daughters of Canaan.
2 - Arise, go to Padanaram, to the house of Bethuel thy mother's father; and take thee a wife from thence of the daughters of Laban thy mother's brother.
3 - <u>And God Almighty bless thee, and make thee fruitful, and multiply thee, that thou mayest be a multitude of people;</u>
4 - <u>And give thee the blessing of Abraham, to thee, and to thy seed with thee; that thou mayest inherit the land wherein thou art a stranger, which God gave unto Abraham.</u>

10 - And Jacob went out from Beersheba, and went toward Haran.
11 - And he lighted upon a certain place, and tarried there all night, because the sun was set; and he took of the stones of that place, and put them for his pillows, and lay down in that place to sleep.

12 - And he dreamed, and behold a ladder set up on the earth, and the top of it reached to heaven: and behold the angels of God ascending and descending on it.
13 And, behold, the LORD stood above it, and said, I am the LORD God of Abraham thy father, and the God of Isaac: the land whereon thou liest, to thee will I give it, and to thy seed;
14 - And thy seed shall be as the dust of the earth, and thou shalt spread abroad to the west, and to the east, and to the north, and to the south: and in thee and in thy seed shall all the families of the earth be blessed.

Deuteronomy 11:23 – 25
23 - Then will the LORD drive out all these nations from before you, and ye shall possess greater nations and mightier than yourselves.
24 - Every place whereon the soles of your feet shall tread shall be yours: from the wilderness and Lebanon, from the river, the river Euphrates, even unto the uttermost sea shall your coast be.
25 - There shall no man be able to stand before you: for the LORD your God shall lay the fear of you and the dread of you upon all the land that ye shall tread upon, as he hath said unto you.

Ezekiel 47:13 – 23
13 - Thus saith the Lord GOD; This shall be the border, whereby ye shall inherit the land according to the twelve tribes of Israel: Joseph shall have two portions.
14 - And ye shall inherit it, one as well as another: concerning the which I lifted up mine hand to give it unto your fathers: and this land shall fall unto you for inheritance.
15 - And this shall be the border of the land toward the north side, from the great sea, the way of Hethlon, as men go to Zedad;
16 - Hamath, Berothah, Sibraim, which is between the border of Damascus and the border of Hamath; Hazarhatticon, which is by the coast of Hauran.
17- And the border from the sea shall be Hazarenan, the border of Damascus, and the north northward, and the border of Hamath. And this is the north side.
18 - And the east side ye shall measure from Hauran, and from Damascus, and from Gilead, and from the land of Israel by Jordan, from the border unto the east sea. And this is the east side.
19 - And the south side southward, from Tamar even to the waters of strife in Kadesh, the river to the great sea. And this is the south side southward.
20 - The west side also shall be the great sea from the border, till a man come over against Hamath. This is the west side.
21 - So shall ye divide this land unto you according to the tribes of Israel.
22 - And it shall come to pass, that ye shall divide it by lot for an inheritance unto you, and to the strangers that sojourn among you, which shall beget children among you: and they shall be unto you as born in the country among the children of Israel; they shall have inheritance with you among the tribes of Israel.
23 - And it shall come to pass, that in what tribe the stranger sojourneth, there shall ye give him his inheritance, saith the Lord GOD.

Through these scriptures we see that the covenant that the LORD made with Abraham covered all the land - north, east, south and west. The rivers that parted out of the garden covered the north, east, south and west.

> *Genesis 2:10 – 14*
> *10 - And a river went out of Eden to water the garden; <u>and from thence it was parted, and became into four heads.</u>*
> *11 - The name of the first is Pison: that is it which compasseth the <u>whole land of Havilah</u>, where there is gold;*
> *12 - And the gold of that land is good: there is bdellium and the onyx stone.*
> *13 - And the name of the second river is Gihon: the same is it that compasseth the <u>whole land</u> of Ethiopia.*
> *14 - And the name of the third river is Hiddekel: that is it which goeth toward the east of Assyria. And the fourth river is Euphrates.*

We note that the covenant that the LORD made with Abraham about the land directly coincides with the flow of the rivers coming out of the garden. He also made covenant with him that all the nations of the earth will be blessed in his seed.

> *Genesis 22:18*
> *<u>And in thy seed shall all the nations of the earth be blessed</u>; because thou hast obeyed my voice.*
>
> *Isaiah 19:23 – 25*
> *23 - In that day shall there be a highway out of Egypt to Assyria, and the Assyrian shall come into Egypt, and the Egyptian into Assyria, and the Egyptians shall serve with the Assyrians.*
> *24 - <u>In that day shall Israel be the third with Egypt and with Assyria, even a blessing in the midst of the land:</u>*
> *25 - <u>Whom the LORD of hosts shall bless, saying, Blessed be Egypt my people, and Assyria the work of my hands, and Israel mine inheritance.</u>*
>
> *Luke 13:29*
> *<u>And they shall come from the east, and from the west, and from the north, and from the south, and shall sit down in the kingdom of God.</u>*

Isaiah prophesied of the fulfillment of this covenant that the LORD had made with Abraham. David spoke of the river that flowed from the city of God - The holy place of the <u>tabernacles</u> of the most High. Abram was referred to by Melchizedek as "Abram of the most high God".

> *Genesis 14:19*
> *And he blessed him, and said, Blessed be Abram of the most high God, possessor of heaven and earth:*

The following scriptures prophesy of the rivers that shall come forth for the healing of the nations.

Psalms 46:4 - 5
4 - There is a river, the streams whereof shall make glad the city of God, the holy place of the tabernacles of the most High.
5 - God is in the midst of her; she shall not be moved: God shall help her, and that right early.

Isaiah 41:18
I will open rivers in high places, and fountains in the midst of the valleys: I will make the wilderness a pool of water, and the dry land springs of water.

Ezekiel 47:1 – 12
1 - Afterward he brought me again unto the door of the house; and, behold, waters issued out from under the threshold of the house eastward: for the forefront of the house stood toward the east, and the waters came down from under from the right side of the house, at the south side of the altar.
2 - Then brought he me out of the way of the gate northward, and led me about the way without unto the utter gate by the way that looketh eastward; and, behold, there ran out waters on the right side.
3 - And when the man that had the line in his hand went forth eastward, he measured a thousand cubits, and he brought me through the waters; the waters were to the ankles.
4 - Again he measured a thousand, and brought me through the waters; the waters were to the knees. Again he measured a thousand, and brought me through; the waters were to the loins.
5 - Afterward he measured a thousand; and it was a river that I could not pass over: for the waters were risen, waters to swim in, a river that could not be passed over.
6 - And he said unto me, Son of man, hast thou seen this? Then he brought me, and caused me to return to the brink of the river.
7 - Now when I had returned, behold, at the bank of the river were very many trees on the one side and on the other.
8 - Then said he unto me, These waters issue out toward the east country, and go down into the desert, and go into the sea: which being brought forth into the sea, the waters shall be healed.
9 - And it shall come to pass, that every thing that liveth, which moveth, whithersoever the rivers shall come, shall live: and there shall be a very great multitude of fish, because these waters shall come thither: for they shall be healed; and every thing shall live whither the river cometh.
10 - And it shall come to pass, that the fishers shall stand upon it from Engedi even unto Eneglaim; they shall be a place to spread forth nets; their fish shall be according to their kinds, as the fish of the great sea, exceeding many.
11 - But the miry places thereof and the marishes thereof shall not be healed; they shall be given to salt.

> *12 - <u>And by the river upon the bank thereof, on this side and on that side, shall grow all trees for meat, whose leaf shall not fade, neither shall the fruit thereof be consumed: it shall bring forth new fruit according to his months, because their waters they issued out of the sanctuary: and the fruit thereof shall be for meat, and the leaf thereof for medicine.</u>*
>
> *Revelation 22:1 – 5*
> *1 - <u>And he shewed me a pure river of water of life, clear as crystal, proceeding out of the throne of God and of the Lamb.</u>*
> *2 - <u>In the midst of the street of it, and on either side of the river, was there the tree of life, which bare twelve manner of fruits, and yielded her fruit every month: and the leaves of the tree were for the healing of the nations.</u>*
> *3 - And there shall be no more curse: but the throne of God and of the Lamb shall be in it; and his servants shall serve him:*
> *4 - And they shall see his face; and his name shall be in their foreheads.*
> *5 - And there shall be no night there; and they need no candle, neither light of the sun; for the Lord God giveth them light: and they shall reign for ever and ever.*

The river came out of Eden to water the garden and from thence became four heads. Through this study we will see that the number four is directly associated with the number of covenants that the LORD made with man. The waters flow eastward to fallen man, and the Lord promised rivers of living water to those who believe on him as the scriptures hath said.

> *John 7:37 – 39*
> *37 - In the last day, that great day of the feast, Jesus stood and cried, saying, If any man thirst, let him come unto me, and drink.*
> *38 - He that believeth on me, as the scripture hath said, out of his belly shall flow rivers of living water.*
> *39 - (But this spake he of the Spirit, which they that believe on him should receive: for the Holy Ghost was not yet given; because that Jesus was not yet glorified.)*

This gospel of Jesus was first preached to Abraham.

> *Galatians 3:8, 13-14, 16, 26-29*
> *8 - <u>And the scripture, foreseeing that God would justify the heathen through faith, preached</u> before the gospel unto Abraham, saying, In thee shall all nations be blessed.*
>
> *13 - Christ hath redeemed us from the curse of the law, being made a curse for us: for it is written, Cursed is every one that hangeth on a tree:*
> *14 - <u>That the blessing of Abraham might come on the Gentiles through Jesus Christ; that we might receive the promise of the Spirit through faith.</u>*
>
> *16 - <u>Now to Abraham and his seed were the promises made. He saith not, And to seeds, as of many; but as of one, And to thy seed, which is Christ.</u>*

> *26 - For ye are all the children of God by faith in Christ Jesus.*
> *27 - For as many of you as have been baptized into Christ have put on Christ.*
> *28 - There is neither Jew nor Greek, there is neither bond nor free, there is neither male nor female: for ye are all one in Christ Jesus.*
> *29 - <u>And if ye be Christ's, then are ye Abraham's seed, and heirs according to the promise.</u>*

To summarize this section, we found through the scriptures that

- The garden is where the tree of life is.
- The river that waters the garden comes out of Eden and breaks off from the garden into four heads.
- The waters flow eastward, and the area of the waters cover all the land and all the people.
- The river has a direct correlation to the covenant that the LORD God made with Abraham
- The covenant pertained to both the natural and the spiritual seed of Abraham.
- That the gospel of faith was first preached to Abraham through covenant.

A HELP MEET

> *Genesis 2:18-20*
> *18 - And the LORD God said, It is not good that the man should be alone; I will make him an help meet for him.*
> *19 - And out of the ground the LORD God formed every beast of the field, and every fowl of the air; and brought them unto Adam to see what he would call them: and whatsoever Adam called every living creature, that was the name thereof.*
> *20 - And Adam gave names to all cattle, and to the fowl of the air, and to every beast of the field; but for Adam there was not found an help meet for him.*

God saw Adam's need for companionship, so he purposed to bring forth a help meet. He formed every beast of the field, and every fowl of the air. He gave Adam the authority to name them. When you name something, it gives you dominion and you give to it its nature. He named every living creature, man is still naming new creatures every day because the seas and the earth are still bringing forth new life. Yet they were not comparable to Adam.

> *Genesis 2:21 – 25*
> *21 - And the LORD God caused a deep sleep to fall upon Adam, and he slept: and he took one of his ribs, and closed up the flesh instead thereof;*
> *22 - And the rib, which the LORD God had taken from man, made he a woman, and brought her unto the man.*
> *23 - And Adam said, This is now bone of my bones, and flesh of my flesh: she shall be called Woman, because she was taken out of Man.*
> *24 - Therefore shall a man leave his father and his mother, and shall cleave unto his wife: and they shall be one flesh.*

25 - And they were both naked, the man and his wife, and were not ashamed.

The LORD God formed a help meet for Adam from the glory that God had given to him. Eve was not the image of God but was the glory of Adam. Paul said that this was a great mystery, for he compared the man and his wife to Christ and the church. Just as Eve was bone of his bone and flesh of his flesh, he said that we are now members of Christ's body. We are of his flesh and of his bones - new creatures in Christ.

1Timothy 2:13
For Adam was first formed, then Eve.

1Corinthians 11:7 - 9
7 - For a man indeed ought not to cover his head, <u>forasmuch as he is the image and glory of God: but the woman is the glory of the man.</u>
8 - <u>For the man is not of the woman; but the woman of the man.</u>
9 - <u>Neither was the man created for the woman; but the woman for the man.</u>

Ephesians 5:22 – 33
22 - Wives, submit yourselves unto your own husbands, as unto the Lord.
23 - For the husband is the head of the wife, even as Christ is the head of the church: and he is the saviour of the body.
24 - <u>Therefore as the church is subject unto Christ, so let the wives be to their own husbands in every thing.</u>
25 - <u>Husbands, love your wives, even as Christ also loved the church, and gave himself for it;</u>
26 - <u>That he might sanctify and cleanse it with the washing of water by the word,</u>
27 - <u>That he might present it to himself a glorious church, not having spot, or wrinkle, or any such thing; but that it should be holy and without blemish.</u>
28 - <u>So ought men to love their wives as their own bodies. He that loveth his wife loveth himself.</u>
29 - <u>For no man ever yet hated his own flesh; but nourisheth and cherisheth it, even as the Lord the church:</u>
30 - <u>For we are members of his body, of his flesh, and of his bones.</u>
31 - <u>For this cause shall a man leave his father and mother, and shall be joined unto his wife, and they two shall be one flesh.</u>
32 - <u>This is a great mystery: but I speak concerning Christ and the church.</u>
33 - Nevertheless let every one of you in particular so love his wife even as himself; and the wife see that she reverence her husband.

The LORD God said that he would give Adam a help meet. God took a rib from Adam's side and closed up the flesh. With the rib he formed the woman and brought her to Adam. Notice that Adam also called her Woman. He was the image of God, therefore, he knew the mind of God and he named her woman also. This sealed the union between Adam and the woman when he called her what God called her. He was able to see her as God saw her - a help meet, comparable to Adam, not beneath. Bone of his bones, flesh of his flesh: someone to be one with, to love and to cherish and be by his side.

> *Genesis 2:22 – 23*
> *22 - And the rib, which the LORD God had taken from man, <u>made he a woman, and brought her unto the man.</u>*
> *23 - And Adam said, This is now bone of my bones, and flesh of my flesh: <u>she shall be called Woman, because she was taken out of Man.</u>*

The ability to name things and give them their nature came from the image of God. We will keep this in mind as we study the next chapter.

THE MYSTERY

Paul made comparison between a man and his wife to Christ and His church. We are members of his body, of his flesh, and of his bones.

> *Ephesians 5:30 – 32*
> *30 - <u>For we are members of his body, of his flesh, and of his bones.</u>*
> *31 - <u>For this cause shall a man leave his father and mother, and shall be joined unto his wife, and they two shall be one flesh.</u>*
> *32 - <u>This is a great mystery: but I speak concerning Christ and the church.</u>*

We see the comparison between the bride of Adam being formed from his side to the bride of the Lamb being formed from His side when we look at the cross.

> *Revelation 21:9*
> *And there came unto me one of the seven angels which had the seven vials full of the seven last plagues, and talked with me, saying, Come hither, <u>I will shew thee the bride, the Lamb's wife.</u>*

> *John 19:33 – 37*
> *33 - <u>But when they came to Jesus, and saw that he was dead already, they brake not his legs:</u>*
> *34 - <u>But one of the soldiers with a spear pierced his side, and forthwith came there out blood and water.</u>*
> *35 - And he that saw it bare record, and his record is true: and he knoweth that he saith true, that ye might believe.*
> *36 - For these things were done, that the scripture should be fulfilled, A bone of him shall not be broken.*
> *37 - And again another scripture saith, <u>They shall look on him whom they pierced.</u>*

When the soldier came to Jesus he was already dead, but he thrust the spear into His side and blood and water came forth. John was the only writer who recorded this. In Revelation that same John wrote of the Lamb's wife. When we search the scriptures, we find that the life is in the blood in the earthly, but the life is in the water in the heavenly. The blood (earthly) came first, the water (spiritual) came next. This completed redemption for both the earthly and the heavenly. The natural man and the spiritual man is complete in him.

Colossians 2:10
And ye are complete in him, which is the head of all principality and power:

Leviticus 17:11
For the life of the flesh is in the blood: and I have given it to you upon the altar to make an atonement for your souls: for it is the blood that maketh an atonement for the soul.

John 4:14
But whosoever drinketh of the water that I shall give him shall never thirst; but the water that I shall give him shall be in him a well of water springing up into everlasting life.

Revelation 21:6
And he said unto me, It is done. I am Alpha and Omega, the beginning and the end. I will give unto him that is athirst of the fountain of the water of life freely.

Revelation 22:1
And he shewed me a pure river of water of life, clear as crystal, proceeding out of the throne of God and of the Lamb.

Revelation 22:17
And the Spirit and the bride say, Come. And let him that heareth say, Come. And let him that is athirst come. And whosoever will, let him take the water of life freely.

When the Lamb of God poured out blood and water from his side his bride was formed. Just like Adam and Eve became one flesh we have become one with Christ. The Lamb's bride, a new creature in Christ.

Ephesians 5:30
For we are members of his body, of his flesh, and of his bones.

Just as Adam and Eve were naked and not ashamed The Lamb has removed our covering of shame and we are once again naked before our husband and God.

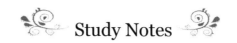

Study Notes

Chapter 3

The Fall

THE BEAST OF THE FIELD

Genesis 3:1
Now the serpent was more subtil than any beast of the field which the LORD God had made. And he said unto the woman, Yea, hath God said, Ye shall not eat of every tree of the garden?

Genesis 2:4 – 6
4 - These are the generations of the heavens and of the earth when they were created, in the day that the LORD God made the earth and the heavens,
5 - And every plant of the field before it was in the earth, and every herb of the field before it grew: for the LORD God had not caused it to rain upon the earth, and there was not a man to till the ground.
6 - But there went up a mist from the earth and watered the whole face of the ground.

We read in Genesis two that God had created the plant of the field and the herb of the field before it grew. The reason stated for this was because there was no need for rain because a mist from the earth watered the face of the ground. God had prepared the seed for the field before there was a man to till it. When we look at this account of the conversation of the serpent and the woman we know that this took place in the garden, the spiritual realm where Adam was placed. Some translations state serpent to mean liar or deceiver. The serpent was a beast of the field. A field is where seed is sown, when God spoke to the serpent in verse fifteen he referred to the serpent's seed. We studied in chapter two that the garden was a place of knowledge. This gives us the understanding that in this scripture that the field was the mind and the seed of the serpent was a lie. This conversation between the serpent and the woman took place in her mind or thoughts. This correlates with the temptation of Jesus in the wilderness.

Matthew 4:1 – 11
1 - Then was Jesus led up of the Spirit into the wilderness to be tempted of the devil.
2 - And when he had fasted forty days and forty nights, he was afterward an hungred.
3 - And when the tempter came to him, he said, If thou be the Son of God, command that these stones be made bread.
4 - But he answered and said, It is written, Man shall not live by bread alone, but by every word that proceedeth out of the mouth of God.
5 - Then the devil taketh him up into the holy city, and setteth him on a pinnacle of the temple,

6 - And saith unto him, If thou be the Son of God, cast thyself down: for it is written, He shall give his angels charge concerning thee: and in their hands they shall bear thee up, lest at any time thou dash thy foot against a stone.
7 - Jesus said unto him, It is written again, Thou shalt not tempt the Lord God.
8 - Again, the devil taketh him up into an exceeding high mountain, and sheweth him all the kingdoms of the world, and the glory of them;
9 - And saith unto him, All these things will I give thee, if thou wilt fall down and worship me.
10 - Then saith Jesus unto him, Get thee hence, Satan: for it is written, Thou shalt worship the Lord thy God, and him only shalt thou serve.
11 - Then the devil leaveth him, and, behold, angels came and ministered unto him.

We read here that Jesus was <u>led up of the Spirit</u> into the wilderness to be tempted of the devil. He was led up, not out, not to be tempted in the natural but in the spirit. A wilderness is a place without inhabitants. Adam was put out of the garden making it a wilderness. This was not a conversation with a natural serpent but a spiritual being in a spiritual place. When comparing the natural or carnal man to the spiritual, Peter and Jude both refer to them as beasts. Ungodly men spreading lies and speaking evil about things they do not understand. Carnally minded and not spiritually minded. Fulfilling the lust of the flesh and not walking after the Spirit.

Romans 8:5 –8
5 - For they that are after the flesh <u>do mind the things of the flesh; but they that are after the Spirit the things of the Spirit.</u>
6 - For to be <u>carnally minded is death; but to be spiritually minded is life and peace.</u>
7 - <u>Because the carnal mind is enmity against God:</u> for it is not subject to the law of God, neither indeed can be.
8 - So then they that are in the flesh cannot please God.

2Peter 2:10 – 12
10 - But chiefly <u>them that walk after the flesh in the lust of uncleanness,</u> and despise government. Presumptuous are they, selfwilled, they are not afraid to speak evil of dignities.
11 - Whereas angels, which are greater in power and might, bring not railing accusation against them before the Lord.
12 - <u>But these, as natural brute beasts</u>, made to be taken and destroyed, <u>speak evil of the things that they understand not;</u> and shall utterly perish in their own corruption;

Jude 1:4
For there are certain men crept in unawares, who were before of old ordained to this condemnation, <u>ungodly men, turning the grace of our God into lasciviousness,</u> and denying the only Lord God, and our Lord Jesus Christ.

Jude 1:10 – 11
10 - But these speak evil of those things which they know not: <u>but what they know naturally, as brute beasts, in those things they corrupt themselves.</u>
11 - Woe unto them! for they have gone in the way of Cain, and ran greedily after the error of Balaam for reward, and perished in the gainsaying of Core.

Jude 1:16
<u>These are murmurers, complainers, walking after their own lusts;</u> and their mouth speaketh great swelling words, having men's persons in admiration because of advantage.

The word says that Jesus was tempted with all the same things that we are tempted with. This statement confirms that this is a spiritual temptation. Satan is a spiritual being and not a natural - the tempter.

Hebrews 4:14 – 15
14 - Seeing then that we have a great high priest, <u>that is passed into the heavens, Jesus the Son of God,</u> let us hold fast our profession.
15 - For we have not an high priest which cannot be touched with the feeling of our infirmities; <u>but was in all points tempted like as we are, yet without sin.</u>

Matthew 4:1 – 3
1 - <u>Then was Jesus led up of the Spirit into the wilderness to be tempted of the devil.</u>
2 - And when he had fasted forty days and forty nights, he was afterward an hungred.
3 - <u>And when the tempter came to him,</u> he said, If thou be the Son of God, command that these stones be made bread.

The field that the tempter exists in is a spiritual and not a natural field. The word says that men sow into a spiritual field. In the spiritual field exists both flesh and the Spirit of life.

Galatians 6:7 – 9
7 - Be not deceived; God is not mocked: for whatsoever a man soweth, that shall he also reap.
8 - <u>For he that soweth to his flesh shall of the flesh reap corruption; but he that soweth to the Spirit shall of the Spirit reap life everlasting.</u>
9 - And let us not be weary in well doing: for in due season we shall reap, if we faint not.

Genesis 6:3
And the LORD said, <u>My spirit shall not always strive with man, for that he also is flesh:</u> yet his days shall be an hundred and twenty years.

Romans 8:1 – 13
1 - There is therefore now no condemnation to them which are in Christ Jesus, who walk not after the flesh, but after the Spirit.
2 - For the law of the Spirit of life in Christ Jesus hath made me free from the law of sin and death.
3 - For what the law could not do, in that it was weak through the flesh, God sending his own Son in the likeness of sinful flesh, and for sin, condemned sin in the flesh:
4 - That the righteousness of the law might be fulfilled in us, who walk not after the flesh, but after the Spirit.
5 - For they that are after the flesh do mind the things of the flesh; but they that are after the Spirit the things of the Spirit.
6 - For to be carnally minded is death; but to be spiritually minded is life and peace.
7 - Because the carnal mind is enmity against God: for it is not subject to the law of God, neither indeed can be.
8 - So then they that are in the flesh cannot please God.
9 - But ye are not in the flesh, but in the Spirit, if so be that the Spirit of God dwell in you. Now if any man have not the Spirit of Christ, he is none of his.
10 - And if Christ be in you, the body is dead because of sin; but the Spirit is life because of righteousness.
11 - But if the Spirit of him that raised up Jesus from the dead dwell in you, he that raised up Christ from the dead shall also quicken your mortal bodies by his Spirit that dwelleth in you.
12 - Therefore, brethren, we are debtors, not to the flesh, to live after the flesh.
13 - For if ye live after the flesh, ye shall die: but if ye through the Spirit do mortify the deeds of the body, ye shall live.

These scriptures confirm that this is a battle in the mind or thoughts as we read in the temptation of the woman. The garden is a place of knowledge where the tree of life and the tree of the knowledge of good and evil exist. Satan is the tempter and the wilderness that Jesus was tempted in was the spirit.

THE TREE OF KNOWLEDGE OF GOOD AND EVIL

The law of sin and death is the tree of the knowledge of good and evil. The righteousness of the law is fulfilled in us and the curse of the law was nailed to the cross.

Romans 3:20
Therefore by the deeds of the law there shall no flesh be justified in his sight: for by the law is the knowledge of sin.

Romans 8:3 - 4
3 - For what the law could not do, in that it was weak through the flesh, God sending his own Son in the likeness of sinful flesh, and for sin, condemned sin in the flesh:

4 - <u>That the righteousness of the law might be fulfilled in us, who walk not after the flesh, but after the Spirit.</u>

Galatians 3:10
<u>For as many as are of the works of the law are under the curse: for it is written, Cursed is every one that continueth not in all things which are written in the book of the law to do them.</u>

Galatians 3:13 – 14
13 - <u>Christ hath redeemed us from the curse of the law, being made a curse for us: for it is written, Cursed is every one that hangeth on a tree:</u>
14 - That the blessing of Abraham might come on the Gentiles through Jesus Christ; <u>that we might receive the promise of the Spirit through faith.</u>

Colossians 2:14
<u>Blotting out the handwriting of ordinances that was against us, which was contrary to us, and took it out of the way, nailing it to his cross;</u>

Galatians reveals that the knowledge of sin was by the law. The curse of the law was the inability to keep the law. Christ redeemed us from the curse of the law so that the righteousness of the law might be fulfilled in us. Walking after the Spirit and not after the flesh, we can fulfill the righteousness of the law. The law is the tree of the knowledge of good and evil, for it reveals the knowledge of sin, blessings and curses. In the garden God made to grow both the tree of life and the tree of the knowledge of good and evil after he placed the man in the garden. LORD God is covenant God, the tree of life and the tree of Knowledge of good and evil are two covenants. Covenants are made in the spirit, for God is a Spirit, they that worship him must worship Him in spirit and in truth. The tree of life is the covenant of faith and the tree of the knowledge of good and evil is the covenant of law. Faith was first preached unto Abraham. The law was given because of transgressions. Therefore, the tree of life is mentioned first before the tree of knowledge of good and evil. Remember that Saul was given as a king to Israel because they had rejected God.

John 4:24
<u>God is a Spirit: and they that worship him must worship him in spirit and in truth.</u>

Galatians 3:8, 16 - 29
8 - <u>And the scripture, foreseeing that God would justify the heathen through faith, preached before the gospel unto Abraham, saying, In thee shall all nations be blessed.</u>

16 - <u>Now to Abraham and his seed were the promises made. He saith not, And to seeds, as of many; but as of one, And to thy seed, which is Christ.</u>
17 - <u>And this I say, that the covenant, that was confirmed before of God in Christ, the law, which was four hundred and thirty years after, cannot disannul, that it should make the promise of none effect.</u>
18 - For if the inheritance be of the law, it is no more of promise: <u>but God gave it to Abraham by promise.</u>

19- Wherefore then serveth the law? It was added because of transgressions, till the seed should come to whom the promise was made; and it was ordained by angels in the hand of a mediator.
20 - Now a mediator is not a mediator of one, but God is one.
21 - Is the law then against the promises of God? God forbid: for if there had been a law given which could have given life, verily righteousness should have been by the law.
22 - But the scripture hath concluded all under sin, that the promise by faith of Jesus Christ might be given to them that believe.
23 - But before faith came, we were kept under the law, shut up unto the faith which should afterwards be revealed.
24 - Wherefore the law was our schoolmaster to bring us unto Christ, that we might be justified by faith.
25 - But after that faith is come, we are no longer under a schoolmaster.
26 - For ye are all the children of God by faith in Christ Jesus.
27 - For as many of you as have been baptized into Christ have put on Christ.
28 - There is neither Jew nor Greek, there is neither bond nor free, there is neither male nor female: for ye are all one in Christ Jesus.
29 - And if ye be Christ's, then are ye Abraham's seed, and heirs according to the promise.

When the promised seed came, the tree of knowledge of good and evil was removed from the garden as we read in Revelations.

Galatians 3:25
But after that faith is come, we are no longer under a schoolmaster.

Revelation 2:7
He that hath an ear, let him hear what the Spirit saith unto the churches; To him that overcometh will I give to eat of the tree of life, which is in the midst of the paradise of God.

THE TREE OF LIFE

Jesus said that it is in the midst of the paradise of God. The tree of life and the tree of knowledge of good and evil grew in the garden where the river flowed out of Eden. After the tree of knowledge of good and evil has been removed it is now the paradise of God. The New Jerusalem. Death cannot abide in paradise, therefore the tree of knowledge of good and evil is removed.

Revelation 22:1 – 5, 14
1 - And he shewed me a pure river of water of life, clear as crystal, proceeding out of the throne of God and of the Lamb.
2 - In the midst of the street of it, and on either side of the river, was there the tree of life, which bare twelve manner of fruits, and yielded her fruit every month: and the leaves of the tree were for the healing of the nations.
3 - And there shall be no more curse: but the throne of God and of the Lamb shall be in it; and his servants shall serve him:
4 - And they shall see his face; and his name shall be in their foreheads.

5 - And there shall be no night there; and they need no candle, neither light of the sun; for the Lord God giveth them light: and they shall reign for ever and ever.

14 - Blessed are they that do His commandments, <u>that they may have right to the tree of life, and may enter in through the gates into the city.</u>

The tree of life is the covenant of faith, the new Jerusalem coming down out of heaven, the Lamb's bride. The curse has been removed and a new covenant has been established upon the apostles of the Lamb. The promises to Abraham sealed into the walls of it.

Revelation 3:12
Him that overcometh will I make a pillar in the temple of my God, and he shall go no more out: and I will write upon him the name of my God, and the name of the city of my God, which is new Jerusalem, which cometh down out of heaven from my God: and I will write upon him my new name.

Revelation 21:2
And I John saw the holy city, new Jerusalem, coming down from God out of heaven, <u>prepared as a bride adorned for her husband.</u>

Revelation 21:9 – 14
9 - And there came unto me one of the seven angels which had the seven vials full of the seven last plagues, and talked with me, saying, Come hither, <u>I will shew thee the bride, the Lamb's wife.</u>
10 - <u>And he carried me away in the spirit to a great and high mountain, and shewed me that great city, the holy Jerusalem, descending out of heaven from God,</u>
11 - Having the glory of God: and her light was like unto a stone most precious, even like a jasper stone, clear as crystal;
12 - <u>And had a wall great and high, and had twelve gates, and at the gates twelve angels, and names written thereon, which are the names of the twelve tribes of the children of Israel:</u>
13 - On the east three gates; on the north three gates; on the south three gates; and on the west three gates.
14 - <u>And the wall of the city had twelve foundations, and in them the names of the twelve apostles of the Lamb.</u>

THE SEED OF THE SERPENT

When the serpent asked the woman hath God said that ye shall not eat of every tree of The garden, he was only referring to the tree of knowledge of good and evil. The only tree that God had commanded Adam not to eat of it. The serpent beguiled the woman, Adam's wife. We have searched the scripture and found that the tree of life represents a covenant of faith and the tree of knowledge of good and evil represents the covenant of the law. Both were present in the garden.

> *Genesis 3:1*
> *Now the serpent was more subtil than any beast of the field which the LORD God had made. And he said unto the woman, <u>Yea, hath God said</u>, Ye shall not eat of every tree of the garden?*

The very words "hath God said" were a seed of doubt placed into the heart of Adam's wife. Scripture states that whatever is not of faith is sin. The serpent's question was full of doubt.

> *Galatians 3:12*
> *<u>And the law is not of faith</u>: but, The man that doeth them shall live in them.*

> *Romans 14:23*
> *And he that doubteth is damned if he eat, because he eateth not of faith: <u>for whatsoever is not of faith is sin.</u>*

The woman's response was not honest. She did not refer to the tree for what it was. She did not identify it as the tree of the knowledge of good and evil. When we do not clearly identify that which God has told us not to eat of we leave room for doubt to come in against God's word. She not only did not identify it she added to it changing the word of God.

> *Genesis 3:2 – 7*
> *2 - And the woman said unto the serpent, We may eat of the fruit of the trees of the garden:*
> *3 - <u>But of the fruit of the tree which is in the midst of the garden, God hath said, Ye shall not eat of it, neither shall ye touch it, lest ye die.</u>*

Therefore, opening the door for disobedience to take hold.

> *4 - And the serpent said unto the woman, <u>Ye shall not surely die:</u>*
> *5 - <u>For God doth know that in the day ye eat thereof, then your eyes shall be opened, and ye shall be as gods, knowing good and evil.</u>*
> *6 - <u>And when the woman saw that the tree was good for food, and that it was pleasant to the eyes, and a tree to be desired to make one wise, she took of the fruit thereof, and did eat, and gave also unto her husband with her; and he did eat.</u>*

Their eyes were open to their nakedness which brought shame. We have already determined that the tree of the knowledge of good and evil is the law. The law was sent to show us how sinful we are, it opens our eyes to ourselves. The knowledge of sin brings shame.

> *7 - <u>And the eyes of them both were opened, and they knew that they were naked; and they sewed fig leaves together, and made themselves aprons.</u>*
>
> *Romans 7:13*
> *Was then that which is good made death unto me? God forbid. <u>But sin, that it might appear sin, working death in me by that which is good; that sin by the commandment might become exceeding sinful.</u>*

THE COVERING

We all have sinned and come short of the glory of God. By faith in Christ Jesus we can be set free from sin and death.

> *Romans 8:2*
> *For the law of the Spirit of life in Christ Jesus hath made me free from the law of sin and death.*

Under the law man gave himself a partial covering for sin, a temporary fix. Just like the fig leaves would die and be replaced the priests would also die and be replaced and the offerings would have to be given continually. Saul was king over Israel under the Levitical law. The law forbids him to offer the sacrifice himself, it had to be done by the priests. Because of his rebellion the kingdom was taken from him and given to another. We read in verse 21 that God made coats of skins and clothed them. These coats of skin would be the law of sacrifice that God would give man to cover sin. This covering would be given through two covenants. The first would be replaced by the second. Jesus would fulfill the Law and provide an eternal covering. Once this eternal covering was established the law would no longer be needed.

> *Genesis 3:21*
> *<u>Unto Adam also and to his wife did the LORD God make coats of skins and clothed them.</u>*
>
> *Hebrews 7:22 – 28*
> *22 - <u>By so much was Jesus made a surety of a better testament.</u>*
> *23 - <u>And they truly were many priests, because they were not suffered to continue by reason of death:</u>*
> *24 - <u>But this man, because he continueth ever,</u> hath an unchangeable priesthood.*
> *25 - Wherefore he is able also to save them to the uttermost that come unto God by him, seeing he ever liveth to make intercession for them.*
> *26 - For such an high priest became us, who is holy, harmless, undefiled, separate from sinners, and made higher than the heavens;*

> *27 - <u>Who needeth not daily, as those high priests, to offer up sacrifice, first for his own sins, and then for the people's: for this he did once, when he offered up himself.</u>*
> *28 - <u>For the law maketh men high priests which have infirmity; but the word of the oath, which was since the law, maketh the Son, who is consecrated for evermore.</u>*

I recommend that you study Hebrews and get a complete understanding of the priesthood of Jesus Christ.

HEARING HIS VOICE

> *Genesis 3:8 – 10*
> *8 - <u>And they heard the voice of the LORD God walking in the garden in the cool of the day: and Adam and his wife hid themselves from the presence of the LORD God amongst the trees of the garden.</u>*
> *9 - And the LORD God called unto Adam, and said unto him, Where art thou?*
> *10 - <u>And he said, I heard thy voice in the garden, and I was afraid, because I was naked; and I hid myself.</u>*

Adam still heard God's voice even after eating of the tree of the knowledge of good and evil. Only now instead of peace and joy it brought fear, separation and shame. Under the law, the children of Israel could not bear to hear the voice of the LORD. Instead of comfort it brought fear, separation and shame. They removed themselves from it. The law brings fear, separation and shame to those who are under it.

> *Exodus 20:18 – 19*
> *18 - And all the people saw the thunderings, and the lightnings, and the noise of the trumpet, and the mountain smoking: and when the people saw it, <u>they removed, and stood afar off.</u>*
> *19 - And they said unto Moses, <u>Speak thou with us, and we will hear: but let not God speak with us, lest we die.</u>*

> *Romans 3:20*
> *Therefore by the deeds of the law there shall no flesh be justified in his sight: <u>for by the law is the knowledge of sin.</u>*

Jesus said that those of faith would hear his voice. His voice would lead them.

> *John 10:1 – 5, 16, 27*
> *1 - Verily, verily, I say unto you, He that entereth not by the door into the sheepfold, but climbeth up some other way, the same is a thief and a robber.*
> *2 - But he that entereth in by the door is the shepherd of the sheep.*
> *3 - To him the porter openeth; <u>and the sheep hear his voice:</u> and he calleth his own sheep by name, and leadeth them out.*
> *4 - And when he putteth forth his own sheep, he goeth before them, and <u>the sheep follow him: for they know his voice.</u>*

5 - And a stranger will they not follow, but will flee from him: <u>for they know not the voice of strangers.</u>

16 - And other sheep I have, which are not of this fold: them also I must bring, <u>and they shall hear my voice;</u> and there shall be one fold, and one shepherd.

27 - <u>My sheep hear my voice,</u> and I know them, and they follow me:

Revelation 3:20
Behold, I stand at the door, and knock: <u>if any man hear my voice,</u> and open the door, I will come in to him, and will sup with him, and he with me.

FEAR BRINGS SHAME

Genesis 3:11 – 13
11 - And he said, Who told thee that thou wast naked? Hast thou eaten of the tree, whereof I commanded thee that thou shouldest not eat?

Shame doesn't come from God, it comes from knowledge of sin. God asked "who told thee?" In other words, "I didn't tell you. Have you eaten of the tree?" The knowledge of good and evil brings fear, separation and shame to those who eat the fruit of it.

12 - And the man said, The woman whom thou gavest to be with me, she gave me of the tree, and I did eat.

Adam immediately shifted the blame. Along with fear, separation and shame the fruit of the tree of the knowledge of good and evil produces blame. He didn't accept responsibility for what he did. The scripture says that the woman gave to her husband with her and he did eat. She didn't sneak it in on him, he ate it with her. Shame will automatically cause us to want to shift blame on someone else. We see this when God confronted Adam of his disobedience.

13 - And the LORD God said unto the woman, What is this that thou hast done? And the woman said, The serpent beguiled me, and I did eat.

She took his example and shifted the blame also. The only one who didn't shift the blame was the serpent. His intention is to cause man to disobey God's voice. We find this throughout the word of God. He twists the word of God and places doubt in the hearts of men to turn them from God.

2Corinthians 4:3 – 4
3 - But if our gospel be hid, it is hid to them that are lost:
4 - In whom the god of this world hath blinded the minds of them which believe not, lest the light of the glorious gospel of Christ, who is the image of God, should shine unto them.

2Corinthians 11:13 – 15
13 - For such are false apostles, deceitful workers, transforming themselves into the apostles of Christ.
14 - And no marvel; <u>for Satan himself is transformed into an angel of light.</u>
<u>15 - Therefore it is no great thing if his ministers also be transformed as the ministers of righteousness; whose end shall be according to their works.</u>

Genesis 3:14
And the LORD God said unto the serpent, Because thou hast done this, thou art cursed above all cattle, and above every beast of the field; upon thy belly shalt thou go, <u>and dust shalt thou eat all the days of thy life:</u>

The serpent would eat dust all the days of his life. The word says that man is dust, therefore, he would forever be seeking out dust to consume with his mouth. We know that the seed of the serpent was lies, deception and doubt. He would use these against man, to keep him from a God that loves them.

John 8:44
Ye are of your father the devil, and the lusts of your father ye will do. He was a murderer from the beginning, <u>and abode not in the truth, because there is no truth in him. When he speaketh a lie, he speaketh of his own: for he is a liar, and the father of it.</u>

Acts 13:10
And said, O full of all subtilty and all mischief, thou child of the devil, thou enemy of all righteousness, wilt thou not cease to pervert the right ways of the Lord?

1Peter 5:8
Be sober, be vigilant; because your adversary the devil, as a roaring lion, walketh about, seeking whom he may devour:

THE ENMITY, THE PROMISED SEED.

> *Genesis 3:15*
> *And I will put enmity between thee and the woman, and between thy seed and her seed; <u>it shall bruise thy head</u>, and <u>thou shalt bruise his heel.</u>*

God made a promise to the serpent that he would bring forth a seed that would take away the power of the enemy. Since the serpent was a liar and the father of it, God was going to bring truth. God said that it would bruise the head of the serpent and the serpent would bruise his heel.

> *John 17:17*
> *Sanctify them through thy truth: <u>thy word is truth.</u>*

> *John 1:1 – 2*
> *1 - In the beginning <u>was the Word</u>, and <u>the Word was with God</u>, and the <u>Word was God.</u>*
> *2 - <u>The same was in the beginning with God.</u>*

> *John 1:14*
> *<u>And the Word was made flesh</u>, and dwelt among us, (and we beheld his glory, the glory as of the only begotten of the Father,) full of grace and truth.*

> *John 14:6*
> *Jesus saith unto him, <u>I am the way, the truth, and the life: no man cometh unto the Father, but by me.</u>*

God's written word is the truth that would bruise the head of the serpent. His word would become flesh and the serpent would bruise his heel. Since a lie separated man from God, truth would reunite them.

> *2Corinthians 5:19*
> *To wit, <u>that God was in Christ, reconciling the world unto himself</u>, not imputing their trespasses unto them; and hath committed unto us <u>the word of reconciliation.</u>*

The only way to be reconciled to God is by truth. Jesus Christ is the truth. The word would come in two covenants; the written word and the word made flesh. The old and the new testaments.

THE FRUIT OF DISOBEDIENCE

> *Genesis 3:16 – 19*
> *16 - Unto the woman he said, I will greatly multiply thy sorrow and thy conception; <u>in sorrow thou shalt bring forth children; and thy desire shall be to thy husband, and he shall rule over thee.</u>*
> *17 - And unto Adam he said, <u>Because thou hast hearkened unto the voice of thy wife, and hast eaten of the tree,</u> of which I commanded thee, saying, Thou shalt not eat of it: <u>cursed is the ground for thy sake; in sorrow shalt thou eat of it all the days of thy life;</u>*
> *18 - Thorns also and thistles shall it bring forth to thee; and thou shalt eat t the herb of the field;*
> *19 - <u>In the sweat of thy face shalt thou eat bread,</u> till thou return unto the ground; for out of it wast thou taken: <u>for dust thou art, and unto dust shalt thou return.</u>*

The relationship between the man and his wife would be affected. The ground would be cursed, and sorrow would be the fruit of their labor, both in child bearing and provision. Labor would be hard, and man would return to dust. We discussed at the beginning of chapter two that man was formed of the dust of the earth. The only way that you can form dust is to mix it with water. Water represents life in the Spirit. Man would lose that spiritual life. He would return to dust, just being of the earth, earthly.

THE PROMISE

> *Genesis 3:20 - 24*
> *20 - And Adam called his wife's name Eve; <u>because she was the mother of all living.</u>*

Adam heard the LORD tell the serpent that a promised seed would come through the woman. She would bring life back to mankind. She would restore man to the covenant God. We will keep this in mind as we search out the covenants of God over the next chapters.

> *21 -Unto Adam also and to his wife did the LORD God make coats of skins, and clothed them.*

As we stated earlier that the coats of skin represent the covenants of God.

> *22 - And the LORD God said, <u>Behold, the man is become as one of us, to know good and evil:</u> and now, lest he put forth his hand, and take also of the tree of life, and eat, and live for <u>ever:</u>*
> *23 - Therefore the LORD God sent him forth from the garden of Eden, to till the ground from whence he was taken.*
> *24 - <u>So he drove out the man; and he placed at the east of the garden of Eden Cherubims, and a flaming sword which turned every way, to keep the way of the tree of life.</u>*

He drove out the man and placed Cherubims and a flaming sword to keep the way of the tree of life. The Cherubims and the flaming sword would represent the two covenants.

> *Exodus 25:18 – 20, 22*
> *18 - And thou shalt make <u>two cherubims of gold</u>, of beaten work shalt thou make them<u>, in the two ends of the mercy seat.</u>*
> *19 - And make one cherub on the one end, and the other cherub on the other end: even of the mercy seat shall ye make the cherubims on the two ends thereof.*
> *20 - And the cherubims shall stretch forth their wings on high, covering the mercy seat with their wings, and their faces shall look one to another; toward the mercy seat shall the faces of the cherubims be.*
>
> *22 - And there I will meet with thee, and I will commune with thee from above the mercy seat, <u>from between the two cherubims which are upon the ark of the testimony, of all things which I will give thee in commandment unto the children of Israel.</u>*

The first covenant would be given upon the mercy seat between the two Cherubims. It would be given by commandment. The second would be given by the Spirit.

> *Ephesians 6:17*
> *And take the helmet of salvation, and <u>the sword of the Spirit, which is the word of God:</u>*

The Cherubims represent the Old Testament covenant and the sword of the Spirit Represents the New Testament covenant.

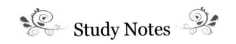

Chapter 4

The Covenant with the Earth

Genesis 3:20
<u>And Adam called his wife's name Eve; because she was the mother of all living.</u>

We ended chapter three with the revelation of the coats of skin, the Cherubims and the flaming sword. With these being covenants that the LORD God would make with man to bring him back to the tree of life. Adam heard the LORD tell the serpent that a promised seed would come through the woman. She would bring life back to mankind. She would bring forth a seed that would restore man to the covenant God. He then called her Eve, the mother of all living. We studied earlier in chapter two that the natural man is spiritually dead because of Adam's disobedience. With these two points in mind we will search out the covenants of God and reveal their mysteries.

THE BLOOD COVENANTS

Genesis 3:21 – 24
21 - Unto Adam also and to his wife did the LORD God make coats of skins, and clothed them.

As we stated earlier that the coats of skin represent the covenants of God. The blood Covering that man would need to be reconciled to a covenant God. The coats covered both the man and the woman.

22 - And <u>the LORD God said, Behold, the man is become as one of us, to know good and evil: and now, lest he put forth his hand, and take also of the tree of life, and eat, and live forever:</u>
23 - Therefore <u>the LORD God sent him forth from the garden of Eden</u>, to till the ground from whence he was taken.
24 - <u>So he drove out the man; and he placed at the east of the garden of Eden Cherubims, and a flaming sword which turned every way, to keep the way of the tree of life.</u>

He drove out the man and placed Cheubims and a flaming sword to keep the way of the tree of life. God's intention is to bring man back to the tree of life. The first thing placed east of the garden of Eden to keep the way of the tree of life was Cherubims. We find Cherubims first mentioned in the making of the mercy seat for the tabernacle of Moses.

Exodus 25:18 – 20, 22
18 - And thou shalt make <u>two cherubims of gold</u>, of beaten work shalt thou make them, <u>in the two ends of the mercy seat.</u>
19 - And make one cherub on the one end, and the other cherub on the other end: even of the mercy seat shall ye make the cherubims on the two ends thereof.

20 - And the cherubims shall stretch forth their wings on high, covering the mercy seat with their wings, and their faces shall look one to another; toward the mercy seat shall the faces of the cherubims be.

22 - And there I will meet with thee, and I will commune with thee from above the mercy seat, <u>from between the two cherubims which are upon the ark of the testimony, of all things which I will give thee in commandment unto the children of Israel.</u>

The covenant of law would be given to Moses upon the mercy seat between the two Cherubims. This giving of the commandments is the first covenant to restore man after Adam was driven out of the garden of Eden. The second would be given with the sword of the Spirit, which is the Word of God. We have already studied that Jesus is the Word of God made flesh.

Ephesians 6:17
And take the helmet of salvation, and <u>the sword of the Spirit, which is the word of God:</u>

The Cherubims represent the Old Testament covenant and the sword of the Spirit represents the New Testament. Both would be confirmed with blood. Both would be represented by tabernacles.

Hebrews 9:1 – 24
1 - <u>Then verily the first covenant had also ordinances of divine service, and a worldly sanctuary.</u>
2 - <u>For there was a tabernacle made;</u> the first, wherein was the candlestick, and the table, and the shewbread; which is called the sanctuary.
3 - <u>And after the second veil, the tabernacle which is called the Holiest of all;</u>
4 - <u>Which had the golden censer, and the ark of the covenant overlaid round about with gold, wherein was the golden pot that had manna, and Aaron's rod that budded, and the tables of the covenant;</u>
5 - <u>And over it the cherubims of glory shadowing the mercyseat; of which we cannot now speak particularly.</u>
6 - Now when these things were thus ordained, the priests went always into the first tabernacle, accomplishing the service of God.
7 - <u>But into the second went the high priest alone once every year, not without blood, which he offered for himself, and for the errors of the people:</u>
8 - <u>The Holy Ghost this signifying, that the way into the holiest of all was not yet made manifest, while as the first tabernacle was yet standing:</u>
9 - <u>Which was a figure for the time then present, in which were offered both gifts and sacrifices, that could not make him that did the service perfect, as pertaining to the conscience;</u>
10 - <u>Which stood only in meats and drinks, and divers washings, and carnal ordinances, imposed on them until the time of reformation.</u>
11 - <u>But Christ being come an high priest of good things to come, by a greater and more perfect tabernacle, not made with hands, that is to say, not of this building;</u>

12 - Neither by the blood of goats and calves, but by His own blood he entered in once into the holy place, having obtained eternal redemption for us.
13 - For if the blood of bulls and of goats, and the ashes of an heifer sprinkling the unclean, sanctifieth to the purifying of the flesh:
14 - How much more shall the blood of Christ, who through the eternal Spirit offered himself without spot to God, purge your conscience from dead works to serve the living God?
15 - And for this cause he is the mediator of the new testament, that by means of death, for the redemption of the transgressions that were under the first testament, they which are called might receive the promise of eternal inheritance.
16 - For where a testament is, there must also of necessity be the death of the testator.
17 - For a testament is of force after men are dead: otherwise it is of no strength at all while the testator liveth.
18 - Whereupon neither the first testament was dedicated without blood.
19 - For when Moses had spoken every precept to all the people according to the law, he took the blood of calves and of goats, with water, and scarlet wool, and hyssop, and sprinkled both the book, and all the people,
20 - Saying, This is the blood of the testament which God hath enjoined unto you.
21 - Moreover he sprinkled with blood both the tabernacle, and all the vessels of the ministry.
22 - And almost all things are by the law purged with blood; and without shedding of blood is no remission.
23 - It was therefore necessary that the patterns of things in the heavens should be purified with these; but the heavenly things themselves with better sacrifices than these.
24 - For Christ is not entered into the holy places made with hands, which are the figures of the true; but into heaven itself, now to appear in the presence of God for us:

Hebrews speaks of the new and better covenant that came through Jesus Christ. Both covenants were dedicated with blood, for without shedding of blood there is no remission of sins. The Cherubims and the flaming sword were placed east of the garden of Eden. When we studied earlier of the river that flowed from Eden and watered the garden, we found the waters flowed east. The river represented covenant and would cover the whole earth – north, east, south and west. From this point we will study the four heads.

Genesis 2:10 – 12
10 - And a river went out of Eden to water the garden; and from thence it was parted, and became into four heads.

This scripture states that the river parted from the garden and became four heads. The word "became" lets us know that this would happen over a period of time.

> *11 - The name of the first is <u>Pison</u>: that is it which compasseth the whole land of Havilah, <u>where there is gold</u>;*
> *12 - <u>And the gold of that land is good</u>: <u>there is bdellium and the onyx stone.</u>*

The first of the four heads, named Pison, which means dispersive. There were three elements that were mentioned in the land that this river would cover. The first gold, which is called good, then bdellium and onyx stone. One interpretation of bdellium is pearl, and onyx is a precious stone. This head would cover all three elements of the land. We will keep this in mind as we search out the first covenant that the LORD God made with man after the fall.

EVE THE MOTHER OF ALL LIVING

We remember that Adam called his wife Eve after he had heard the LORD God tell her that she would bring forth a seed that would bruise the head of the serpent. Eve means living, for she was the mother of all living. With this in mind we will look at the sons of Eve. Notice that the scripture says that he drove the man out. The woman would remain in the covenant with the LORD to bring forth a seed.

> *Genesis 3:20*
> *<u>And Adam called his wife's name Eve; because she was the mother of all living.</u>*

> *Genesis 3:24*
> *<u>So he drove out the man;</u> and he placed at the east of the garden of Eden Cherubims, and a flaming sword which turned every way, to keep the way of the tree of life.*

> *Genesis 4:1*
> *And Adam knew Eve his wife; and she conceived, and bare Cain, <u>and said, I have gotten a man from the LORD.</u>*

We will pay attention to Eve's words that she spoke. I have gotten a man from the LORD. We know that LORD speaks of covenant God. She knew that God had promised her a seed but she referred to Cain as a man.

> *Genesis 4:2*
> *And she again bare his brother Abel. And Abel was a keeper of sheep, <u>but Cain was a tiller of the ground.</u>*

This scripture reveals that Cain was a tiller of the ground. When we first looked at the Garden of Eden, we read that the plant of the field and the herb of the field had not been given because it had not rained upon the earth.

> *Genesis 2:4 – 6*
> *4 - These are the generations of the heavens and of the earth when they were created, in the day that the LORD God made the earth and the heavens,*

> *5 - <u>And every plant of the field before it was in the earth, and every herb of the field before it grew: for the LORD God had not caused it to rain upon the earth, and there was not a man to till the ground.</u>*
> *6 - <u>But there went up a mist from the earth, and watered the whole face of the ground.</u>*

This confirms that Cain would be a type or pattern of a covenant that the LORD God would make with man after it rains. The first mention of rain and a man planting a field was with Noah. Noah was also the first man that the LORD God made covenant with. The covenant that the LORD made with Noah would reverse the curse on the ground that the LORD God gave to Adam. For the LORD said " I do set my bow in the cloud, <u>and it shall be for a token of a covenant between me and the earth.</u>" The first covenant the LORD God would make with man would be between him and the earth.

TILLER OF THE GROUND

> *Genesis 5:28 – 29*
> *28 - And Lamech lived an hundred eighty and two years, and begat a son:*
> *29 - <u>And he called his name Noah, saying, This same shall comfort us concerning our work and toil of our hands, because of the ground which the LORD hath cursed.</u>*
>
> *Genesis 6:5 – 10, 17 – 22*
> *5 - <u>And GOD saw that the wickedness of man was great in the earth, and that every imagination of the thoughts of his heart was only evil continually.</u>*
> *6 - <u>And it repented the LORD that he had made man on the earth, and it grieved him at his heart.</u>*
> *7 - And the LORD said, I will destroy man whom I have created from the face of the earth; both man, and beast, and the creeping thing, and the fowls of the air; for it repenteth me that I have made them.*
> *8 - <u>But Noah found grace in the eyes of the LORD.</u>*
> *9 - These are the generations of Noah: Noah was a just man and perfect in his generations, <u>and Noah walked with God.</u>*
> *10 - And Noah begat three sons, Shem, Ham, and Japheth.*

As his father prophesied Noah would bring comfort. He found grace in the eyes of the LORD, the God of covenant. He would bring covenant to man, the first river head. Notice that the scripture says that Noah walked with God, not LORD God.

> *17 - And, behold, I, even I<u>, do bring a flood of waters upon the earth</u>, <u>to destroy all flesh</u>, wherein is the breath of life, from under heaven; <u>and every thing that is in the earth shall die.</u>*
> *18 - <u>But with thee will I establish my covenant; and thou shalt come into the ark, thou, and thy sons, and thy wife, and thy sons' wives with thee.</u>*
> *19 - And of every living thing of all flesh, two of every sort shalt thou bring into the ark, to keep them alive with thee; they shall be male and female.*
> *20 - Of fowls after their kind, and of cattle after their kind, of every creeping thing of the earth after his kind, two of every sort shall come unto thee, to keep them alive.*

21 - And take thou unto thee of all food that is eaten, and thou shalt gather it to thee; and it shall be for food for thee, and for them.
22 - Thus did Noah; according to all <u>that God commanded him</u>, so did he.

Genesis 7:12
<u>*And the rain*</u> *was upon the earth forty days and forty nights.*

We look at the first river head Pison which means dispersive and we see the correlation between the name of the river and the blessing of Noah's sons. This river would cover all the land where three elements would be. These three elements would represent the three nations that would come from Noah's sons. Noah was the first tiller of the ground, the first husbandman.

Genesis 9:7 – 13
7 - <u>And you, be ye fruitful, and multiply; bring forth abundantly in the earth, and multiply therein.</u>
8 - <u>And God spake unto Noah, and to his sons with him, saying,</u>
9 - <u>And I, behold, I establish my covenant with you, and with your seed after you;</u>
10 - <u>And with every living creature that is with you, of the fowl, of the cattle, and of every beast of the earth with you; from all that go out of the ark, to every beast of the earth.</u>
11 - <u>And I will establish my covenant with you; neither shall all flesh be cut off any more by the waters of a flood; neither shall there any more be a flood to destroy the earth.</u>
12 - <u>And God said, This is the token of the covenant which I make between me and you and every living creature that is with you, for perpetual generations:</u>
13 - I do set my bow in the cloud, <u>and it shall be for a token of a covenant between me and the earth.</u>

Genesis 9:19 – 20
19 - <u>These are the three sons of Noah: and of them was the whole earth overspread.</u>
20 - <u>And Noah began to be an husbandman, and he planted a vineyard:</u>

We see that Noah had become the first husbandman to plant a field, after which he became drunk with the wine of the vineyard. Ham saw his father's nakedness and instead of providing a covering he told his two brothers. Noah was angry and cursed Ham's son. This would set into play the order of the nations.

THE NATIONS DISPERSED

Gen 9:25 – 27
25 - And he said, <u>Cursed be Canaan; a servant of servants shall he be unto his brethren.</u>
26 - And he said, <u>Blessed be the LORD God of Shem; and Canaan shall be his servant.</u>
27 - <u>God shall enlarge Japheth, and he shall dwell in the tents of Shem; and Canaan shall be his servant.</u>

Genesis 10:32
<u>*These are the families of the sons of Noah, after their generations, in their nations: and by these were the nations divided in the earth after the flood.*</u>

Japheth (Gentiles)

Genesis 10:1 - 5
1 - Now these are the generations of the sons of Noah, Shem, Ham, and Japheth: and unto them were sons born after the flood.
2 - The sons of Japheth; Gomer, and Magog, and Madai, and Javan, and Tubal, and Meshech, and Tiras.
3 - And the sons of Gomer; Ashkenaz, and Riphath, and Togarmah.
4 - And the sons of Javan; Elishah, and Tarshish, Kittim, and Dodanim.
5 - <u>By these were the isles of the Gentiles divided in their lands; every one after his tongue, after their families, in their nations.</u>

Ham (Egyptians)

Genesis 10:6 – 20
6 - And the sons of Ham; Cush, and Mizraim, and Phut, and Canaan.
7 - And the sons of Cush; Seba, and Havilah, and Sabtah, and Raamah, and Sabtecha: and the sons of Raamah; Sheba, and Dedan.
8 - And Cush begat Nimrod: he began to be a mighty one in the earth.
9 - He was a mighty hunter before the LORD: wherefore it is said, Even as Nimrod the mighty hunter before the LORD.
10 - And the beginning of his kingdom was Babel, and Erech, and Accad, and Calneh, in the land of Shinar.
11 - Out of that land went forth Asshur, and builded Nineveh, and the city Rehoboth, and Calah,
12 - And Resen between Nineveh and Calah: the same is a great city.
13 - And Mizraim begat Ludim, and Anamim, and Lehabim, and Naphtuhim,
14 - And Pathrusim, and Casluhim, (out of whom came Philistim,) and Caphtorim.
15 - And Canaan begat Sidon his firstborn, and Heth,
16 - And the Jebusite, and the Amorite, and the Girgasite,
17 - And the Hivite, and the Arkite, and the Sinite,

18 - And the Arvadite, and the Zemarite, and the Hamathite: and afterward were the families of the Canaanites spread abroad.
as thou goest, unto Sodom, and Gomorrah, and Admah, and Zeboim, even unto Lasha.
19 - And the border of the Canaanites was from Sidon, as thou comest to Gerar, unto Gaza; as thou goest, unto Sodom, and Gomorrah, and Admah, and Zeboim, even unto Lasha.
20 - These are the sons of Ham, after their families, after their tongues, in their countries, and in their nations.

Psalms 78:51
And smote all the firstborn <u>in Egypt</u>; the chief of their strength in the <u>tabernacles of Ham:</u>

Psalms 105:23
Israel also came <u>into Egypt</u>; and Jacob sojourned in the <u>land of Ham.</u>

Psalms 105:27
They shewed his signs among them, and wonders <u>in the land of Ham.</u>

Psalms 106:22
Wondrous works <u>in the land of Ham</u>, and terrible things <u>by the Red sea.</u>

<u>Shem (Israelites)</u>

Genesis 10:21 – 31
21 - to Shem also, the father of all the children of Eber, the brother of Japheth the elder, even to him were children born.
22 - The children of Shem; Elam, and Asshur, and Arphaxad, and Lud, and Aram.
23 - And the children of Aram; Uz, and Hul, and Gether, and Mash.
24 - And Arphaxad begat Salah; and Salah begat Eber.
25 - And unto Eber were born two sons: the name of one was Peleg; for in his days was the earth divided; and his brother's name was Joktan.
26 - And Joktan begat Almodad, and Sheleph, and Hazarmaveth, and Jerah,
27 - And Hadoram, and Uzal, and Diklah,
28 - And Obal, and Abimael, and Sheba,
29 - And Ophir, and Havilah, and Jobab: all these were the sons of Joktan.
30 - And their dwelling was from Mesha, as thou goest unto Sephar a mount of the east.
31 - These are the sons of Shem, after their families, after their tongues, in their lands, after their nations.

1Chronicles 1:17 – 27
17 - <u>The sons of Shem</u>; Elam, and Asshur, and Arphaxad, and Lud, and Aram, and Uz, and Hul, and Gether, and Meshech.
18 - And Arphaxad begat Shelah, and Shelah begat Eber.
19 - And unto Eber were born two sons: the name of the one was Peleg; because in his days the earth was divided: and his brother's name was Joktan.

20 - And Joktan begat Almodad, and Sheleph, and Hazarmaveth, and Jerah,
21 - Hadoram also, and Uzal, and Diklah,
22 - And Ebal, and Abimael, and Sheba,
23 - And Ophir, and Havilah, and Jobab. All these were the sons of Joktan.
24 - Shem, Arphaxad, Shelah,
25 - Eber, Peleg, Reu,
26 - Serug, Nahor, Terah,
27 - <u>Abram; the same is Abraham.</u>

Three nations would cover the earth, the Assyrians, the Egyptians and the Israelites. Fulfilling the word of prophecy that Noah gave to his sons. Prophesied by Isaiah and fulfilled by Christ.

Genesis 9:25 – 27
25 - And he said, <u>Cursed be Canaan; a servant of servants shall he be unto his brethren.</u>
26 - And he said, <u>Blessed be the LORD God of Shem</u>; and <u>Canaan shall be his servant.</u>
27 - <u>God shall enlarge Japheth, and he shall dwell in the tents of Shem; and Canaan shall be his servant.</u>

Canaan would be the servant of Shem and Japheth would dwell in the tents of Shem. Thus, bringing all three nations together in the tents of Shem. The LORD God would establish his covenant with the house of Shem.

Isaiah 19:23 – 25
23 - In that day shall there be a highway out of <u>Egypt to Assyria, and the Assyrian shall come into Egypt, and the Egyptian into Assyria, and the Egyptians shall serve with the Assyrians.</u>
24 - In that day shall <u>Israel be the third with Egypt and with Assyria, even a blessing in the midst of the land:</u>
25 - Whom the LORD of hosts shall bless, saying, <u>Blessed be Egypt my people, and Assyria the work of my hands, and Israel mine inheritance.</u>

Galatians 3:13 – 16, 29
13 - <u>Christ hath redeemed us from the curse of the law, being made a curse for us: for it is written, Cursed is every one that hangeth on a tree:</u>
14 - <u>That the blessing of Abraham might come on the Gentiles through Jesus Christ; that we might receive the promise of the Spirit through faith.</u>
15 - Brethren, I speak after the manner of men; Though it be but a man's covenant, yet if it be confirmed, no man disannulleth, or addeth thereto.
16 - <u>Now to Abraham and his seed were the promises made. He saith not, And to seeds, as of many; but as of one, And to thy seed, which is Christ.</u>

29 - <u>And if ye be Christ's, then are ye Abraham's seed, and heirs according to the promise.</u>

The three elements that would be in the land were gold, bdellium (pearls) and onyx stone (precious stones).

> *Genesis 2:11 – 12*
> *11 - The name of the first is <u>Pison</u>: that is it which compasseth the whole land of Havilah, <u>where there is gold</u>;*
> *12 - <u>And the gold of that land is good: there is bdellium and the onyx stone.</u>*

We see these three elements in the New Jerusalem coming out of heaven.

> *Revelation 21:18 – 27*
> *18 - And the building of the wall of it was of jasper: and <u>the city was pure gold</u>, like unto clear glass.*
> *19 - <u>And the foundations of the wall of the city were garnished with all manner of precious stones.</u> The first foundation was jasper; the second, sapphire; the third, a chalcedony; the fourth, an emerald;*
> *20 - The fifth, sardonyx; the sixth, sardius; the seventh, chrysolite; the eighth, beryl; the ninth, a topaz; the tenth, a chrysoprasus; the eleventh, a jacinth; the twelfth, an amethyst.*
> *21 - <u>And the twelve gates were twelve pearls; every several gate was of one pearl</u>: and the street of the city was pure gold, as it were transparent glass.*
> *22 - And I saw no temple therein: for the Lord God Almighty and the Lamb are the temple of it.*
> *23 - And the city had no need of the sun, neither of the moon, to shine in it: for the glory of God did lighten it, and the Lamb is the light thereof.*
> *24 - And the nations of them which are saved shall walk in the light of it: and the kings of the earth do bring their glory and honour into it.*
> *25 - And the gates of it shall not be shut at all by day: for there shall be no night there.*
> *26 - And they shall bring the glory and honour of the nations into it.*
> *27 - And there shall in no wise enter into it any thing that defileth, neither whatsoever worketh abomination, or maketh a lie: but they which are written in the Lamb's book of life.*

Through these scriptures we can see that Cain is a type of the covenant that God made with the earth to never curse it again or smite any more every living thing.

> *Genesis 8:20 – 22*
> *20 - And Noah builded an altar unto the LORD; and took of every clean beast, and of every clean fowl, and offered burnt offerings on the altar.*
> *21 - And the LORD smelled a sweet savour; <u>and the LORD said in his heart, I will not again curse the ground any more for man's sake; for the imagination of man's heart is evil from his youth; neither will I again smite any more every thing living, as I have done.</u>*
> *22 - <u>While the earth remaineth, seedtime and harvest, and cold and heat, and summer and winter, and day and night shall not cease.</u>*

DRIVEN FROM THE EARTH

We also see that Cain is a type of the un-regenerated man. A man who wanted to be accepted by his own works. The unsaved.

> *Titus 3:5*
> *Not by works of righteousness which we have done, but according to his mercy he saved us, by the washing of regeneration, and renewing of the Holy Ghost;*
>
> *Genesis 4:3 – 16*
> *3 - And in process of time it came to pass, that Cain brought of the fruit of the ground an offering unto the LORD.*
> *4 - And Abel, he also brought of the firstlings of his flock and of the fat thereof. And the LORD had respect unto Abel and to his offering:*
> *5 - But unto Cain and to his offering he had not respect. And Cain was very wroth, and his countenance fell.*
> *6 - And the LORD said unto Cain, Why art thou wroth? and why is thy countenance fallen?*
> *7 - If thou doest well, shalt thou not be accepted? and if thou doest not well, sin lieth at the door. And unto thee shall be his desire, and thou shalt rule over him.*
> *8 - And Cain talked with Abel his brother: and it came to pass, when they were in the field, that Cain rose up against Abel his brother, and slew him.*
> *9 - And the LORD said unto Cain, Where is Abel thy brother? And he said, I know not: Am I my brother's keeper?*
> *10 - And he said, What hast thou done? the voice of thy brother's blood crieth unto me from the ground.*
> *11 - And now art thou cursed from the earth, which hath opened her mouth to receive thy brother's blood from thy hand;*
> *12 - When thou tillest the ground, it shall not henceforth yield unto thee her strength; a fugitive and a vagabond shalt thou be in the earth.*
> *13 - And Cain said unto the LORD, My punishment is greater than I can bear.*
> *14 - Behold, thou hast driven me out this day from the face of the earth; and from thy face shall I be hid; and I shall be a fugitive and a vagabond in the earth; and it shall come to pass, that every one that findeth me shall slay me.*
> *15 - And the LORD said unto him, Therefore whosoever slayeth Cain, vengeance shall be taken on him sevenfold. And the LORD set a mark upon Cain, lest any finding him should kill him.*
> *16 - And Cain went out from the presence of the LORD, and dwelt in the land of Nod, on the east of Eden.*

Cain went out from the presence of the LORD to the east of Eden. We can never stand in The presence of God with our own works. Just as the children of Israel turned to their own works and wouldn't come into the presence of the LORD. They murdered their brother and would not come to the truth. David wrote about it in Psalms 106.

Psalms 106:39
Thus were they defiled with their own works, and went a whoring with their own inventions.

1John 3:15
15 - Whosoever hateth his brother is a murderer: and ye know that no murderer hath eternal life abiding in him.

John 3:19 – 21
19 - And this is the condemnation, that light is come into the world, and men loved darkness rather than light, because their deeds were evil.
20 - For every one that doeth evil hateth the light, neither cometh to the light, lest his deeds should be reproved.
21 - But he that doeth truth cometh to the light, that his deeds may be made manifest, that they are wrought in God.

John 8:44
Ye are of your father the devil, and the lusts of your father ye will do. He was a murderer from the beginning, and abode not in the truth, because there is no truth in him. When he speaketh a lie, he speaketh of his own: for he is a liar, and the father of it.

Just as Cain slew Abel, the children of the wicked one slew Jesus their brother in the field which is the earth. Jude compared the unsaved to Cain.

1John 3:12
Not as Cain, who was of that wicked one, and slew his brother. And wherefore slew he him? Because his own works were evil, and his brother's righteous.

Jude 1:11
Woe unto them! for they have gone in the way of Cain.

When we read the parable of the wheat and the tares we see the correlation between Cain and the children of the wicked one (un-regenerated man).

Matthew 13:24 – 30, 36 – 43
24 - Another parable put He forth unto them, saying, The kingdom of heaven is likened unto a man which sowed good seed in his field:
25 - But while men slept, his enemy came and sowed tares among the wheat, and went his way.
26 - But when the blade was sprung up, and brought forth fruit, then appeared the tares also.
27 - So the servants of the householder came and said unto him, Sir, didst not thou sow good seed in thy field? from whence then hath it tares?
28 - He said unto them, An enemy hath done this. The servants said unto him, Wilt thou then that we go and gather them up?
29 - But he said, Nay; lest while ye gather up the tares, ye root up also the wheat with them.

30 - Let both grow together until the harvest: and in the time of harvest I will say to the reapers, Gather ye together first the tares, and bind them in bundles to burn them: but gather the wheat into my barn.

36 - Then Jesus sent the multitude away, and went into the house: and his disciples came unto him, saying, Declare unto us the parable of the tares of the field.
37 - He answered and said unto them, <u>He that soweth the good seed is the Son of man;</u>
38 - <u>The field is the world; the good seed are the children of the kingdom; but the tares are the children of the wicked one;</u>
39 - <u>The enemy that sowed them is the devil; the harvest is the end of the world; and the reapers are the angels.</u>
40 - <u>As therefore the tares are gathered and burned in the fire; so shall it be in the end of this world.</u>
41 - <u>The Son of man shall send forth his angels, and they shall gather out of his kingdom all things that offend, and them which do iniquity;</u>
42 - <u>And shall cast them into a furnace of fire: there shall be wailing and gnashing of teeth.</u>
43 - <u>Then shall the righteous shine forth as the sun in the kingdom of their Father. Who hath ears to hear, let him hear.</u>

In this parable Jesus said that the tares (children of the wicked one) shall be gathered and burned in the fire. In the following scriptures we see that the wicked will be cut off from the earth as Cain was.

Genesis 4:11, 14
11 - <u>And now art thou cursed from the earth, which hath opened her mouth to receive thy brother's blood from thy hand;</u>

14 - <u>Behold, thou hast driven me out this day from the face of the earth; and from thy face shall I be hid;</u>

Psalm 37:7 – 11
7 - Rest in the LORD, and wait patiently for him: fret not thyself because of him who prospereth in his way, because of the man who bringeth wicked devices to pass.
8 - Cease from anger, and forsake wrath: fret not thyself in any wise to do evil.
9 - <u>For evildoers shall be cut off: but those that wait upon the LORD, they shall inherit the earth.</u>
10 - <u>For yet a little while, and the wicked shall not be: yea, thou shalt diligently consider his place, and it shall not be.</u>
11 - <u>But the meek shall inherit the earth;</u> and shall delight themselves in the abundance of peace.

Psalms 37:22, 28, 38
22 - <u>For such as be blessed of him shall inherit the earth; and they that be cursed of him shall be cut off.</u>

28 - <u>For the LORD loveth judgment, and forsaketh not his saints; they are preserved for ever: but the seed of the wicked shall be cut off.</u>

38 - <u>But the transgressors shall be destroyed together: the end of the wicked shall be cut off.</u>

Psalms 75:10
<u>*All the horns of the wicked also will I cut off; but the horns of the righteous shall be exalted.*</u>

Proverbs 2:21 – 22
21 - <u>For the upright shall dwell in the land, and the perfect shall remain in it.</u>
22 - <u>But the wicked shall be cut off from the earth, and the transgressors shall be rooted out of it.</u>

Proverbs 10:30
<u>*The righteous shall never be removed: but the wicked shall not inhabit the earth.*</u>

Psalms 125:1
A Song of degrees. <u>They that trust in the LORD shall be as mount Zion, which cannot be removed, but abideth for ever.</u>

Matthew 5:5
<u>*Blessed are the meek: for they shall inherit the earth.*</u>

Cain is a type or pattern of the covenant that The LORD made with Noah that he would never again destroy the earth for the wickedness of man. Just as Cain was cursed from the earth and driven from it, those who do not receive the blood of Jesus will be removed from it. The blood of their brother cries out to the LORD God of covenant.

Genesis 4:10 – 11
10 - And he said, What hast thou done? <u>the voice of thy brother's blood crieth unto me from the ground.</u>
11 - <u>And now art thou cursed from the earth, which hath opened her mouth to receive thy brother's blood from thy hand;</u>

Study Notes

Chapter 5

The Covenant of Abraham

Genesis 9:26
And he said, Blessed be the <u>LORD God of Shem</u>; and Canaan shall be his servant.

1Chronicles 1:17 – 27
17 - <u>The sons of Shem</u>; Elam, and Asshur, and Arphaxad, and Lud, and Aram, and Uz, and Hul, and Gether, and Meshech.
18 - And Arphaxad begat Shelah, and Shelah begat Eber.
19 - And unto Eber were born two sons: the name of the one was Peleg; because in his days the earth was divided: and his brother's name was Joktan.
20 - And Joktan begat Almodad, and Sheleph, and Hazarmaveth, and Jerah,
21 - Hadoram also, and Uzal, and Diklah,
22 - And Ebal, and Abimael, and Sheba,
23 - And Ophir, and Havilah, and Jobab. All these were the sons of Joktan.
24 - Shem, Arphaxad, Shelah,
25 - Eber, Peleg, Reu,
26 - Serug, Nahor, Terah,
27 - <u>Abram; the same is Abraham.</u>

We studied in chapter four the covenant that the LORD made with the earth through Noah. This covenant was the first river head that came out of the Garden of Eden. Noah blessed his son Shem and prophesied of the covenant that would come through his descendants. We studied earlier that LORD God refers to covenant God. Noah blessed the covenant God of Shem. Abram was a son of Shem, the same is Abraham. When we look at the second river head coming out of the Garden of Eden, we see the direct connection with the covenant with Abraham.

Genesis 12:1 – 3, 10 – 13
1 - <u>Now the LORD had said unto Abram</u>, Get thee out of thy country, and from thy kindred, and from thy father's house, unto a land that I will shew thee:
2 - <u>And I will make of thee a great nation,</u> and I will bless thee, and make thy name great; and thou shalt be a blessing:
3 - And I will bless them that bless thee, and curse him that curseth thee: <u>and in thee shall all families of the earth be blessed.</u>

10 - <u>And a river went out of Eden to water the garden; and from thence it was parted, and became into four heads.</u>
11 - The name of the first is Pison: that is it which compasseth the whole land of Havilah, where there is gold;
12 - And the gold of that land is good: there is bdellium and the onyx stone.

> *13 - <u>And the name of the second river is Gihon:</u> the same is it that compasseth the whole land of Ethiopia.*

The name of the first river is Pison which means dispersive. The second is Gihon which means bursting forth. These are referred to as heads. The first river head is directly connected to Noah, the first covenant that the LORD God made. The second would be with a man named Abram. We are going to do a study of this covenant.

> *Genesis 12:1 – 3*
> *1 - <u>Now the LORD had said unto Abram, Get thee out of thy country, and from thy kindred, and from thy father's house, unto a land that I will shew thee:</u>*
> *2 - <u>And I will make of thee a great nation, and I will bless thee,</u> and make thy name great; and thou shalt be a blessing:*
> *3 - <u>And I will bless them that bless thee, and curse him that curseth thee: and in thee shall all families of the earth be blessed.</u>*

Out of the descendants of Shem the LORD chose a man named Abram. He called him out and told him that he would bless him. The fulfilling of the blessing would be determined by his willingness to follow and obey. This began the bursting forth of the LORD God's covenant with fallen man. The covenant with Noah was between God and the earth, but the covenant with Abram would be with man.

> *Genesis 9:13*
> *I do set my bow in the cloud, and it shall be for <u>a token of a covenant between me and the earth.</u>*

> *Genesis 22:18*
> *<u>And in thy seed</u> shall all the nations of the earth be blessed; because thou hast obeyed my voice.*

> *Exodus 2:24*
> *And God heard their groaning, and God remembered his covenant with <u>Abraham</u>, with <u>Isaac</u>, and with <u>Jacob</u>.*

Abraham's covenant would be a two-fold covenant.

PROMISE OF THE EARTH

> *Genesis 13:14 – 17*
> *14 - And the LORD said unto Abram, after that Lot was separated from him, Lift up now thine eyes, and look from the place where thou art <u>northward, and southward, and eastward, and westward:</u>*
> *15 - <u>For all the land which thou seest, to thee will I give it, and to thy seed for ever.</u>*
> *16 - <u>And I will make thy seed as the dust of the earth:</u> so that if a man can number the dust of the earth, then shall thy seed also be numbered.*
> *17 - <u>Arise, walk through the land in the length of it and in the breadth of it; for I will give it unto thee.</u>*

When we studied the river that came out of the Garden of Eden we found that it would cover all the earth (north, east, south and west). This would be a covenant that would come forth. The dust of the earth refers to the earthly man. The first promise of covenant that the LORD made with Abram was with his natural seed. Abram currently had no children because Sarai, his wife was barren. This would only happen by faith. The LORD promised all the land to Abram and his seed by faith.

> *Genesis 15:1 – 7*
> *1 - After these things the word of the LORD came unto Abram in a vision, saying, Fear not, Abram: I am thy shield, and thy exceeding great reward.*
> *2 - <u>And Abram said, Lord GOD, what wilt thou give me, seeing I go childless,</u> and the steward of my house is this Eliezer of Damascus?*
> *3 - And Abram said, Behold, to me thou hast given no seed: and, lo, one born in my house is mine heir.*
> *4 - <u>And, behold, the word of the LORD came unto him, saying, This shall not be thine heir; but he that shall come forth out of thine own bowels shall be thine heir.</u>*
> *5 - And he brought him forth abroad, and said, <u>Look now toward heaven, and tell the stars, if thou be able to number them: and he said unto him, So shall thy seed be.</u>*
> *6 - <u>And he believed in the LORD; and he counted it to him for righteousness.</u>*
> *7 - And he said unto him, I am the LORD that brought thee out of Ur of the Chaldees, <u>to give thee this land to inherit it.</u>*

As we studied in chapter four the first covenant that God made was with the earth. This new covenant that the LORD God will make with a man named Abram will include all the earth. Notice that when speaking to Abram that the LORD said <u>I will give it.</u> The words <u>I will</u> denote a future promise. We also see in this scripture setting that Abram referred to him as Lord GOD, emphasis is on GOD rather than LORD. This was a promise of covenant if Abram would obey his voice. Both his earthly seed and his heavenly would be included in this promise.

THE POSSESSOR OF HEAVEN AND EARTH

The first promise that the LORD made to Abram was concerning his seed being as the dust of the earth. We understand that this pertains to his earthly seed. The second promise referred to stars (this is a heavenly seed). Something took place between the promise of the earthly and the heavenly. We will investigate the scriptures and find out what it was.

> *Genesis 14:1 – 2, 11 – 12, 14 - 17*
> *1 - And it came to pass in the days of Amraphel king of Shinar, Arioch king of Ellasar, Chedorlaomer king of Elam, and Tidal king of nations;*
> *2 - <u>That these made war with Bera king of Sodom, and with Birsha king of Gomorrah,</u> Shinab king of Admah, and Shemeber king of Zeboiim, and the king of Bela, which is Zoar.*
>
> *11 - And they took all the goods of Sodom and Gomorrah, and all their victuals, and went their way.*
> *12 - <u>And they took Lot, Abram's brother's son, who dwelt in Sodom, and his goods, and departed.</u>*
>
> *14 - And when Abram heard that his brother was taken captive, he armed his trained servants, born in his own house, three hundred and eighteen, and pursued them unto Dan.*
> *15 - And he divided himself against them, he and his servants, by night, and smote them, and pursued them unto Hobah, which is on the left hand of Damascus.*
> *16 - <u>And he brought back all the goods, and also brought again his brother Lot, and his goods, and the women also, and the people.</u>*
> *17 - <u>And the king of Sodom went out to meet him after his return from the slaughter of Chedorlaomer, and of the kings that were with him, at the valley of Shaveh, which is the king's dale.</u>*

Abram had been brought word that Sodom and Gomorrah had been defeated and the people taken captive. Among the captives was Lot. Abram took his men and went against the four kings and defeated them. He then brought back the people and the goods. When the king of Sodom heard this, he went out to meet Abram in the Valley of the Kings. Yet another king met with Abram there.

> *Genesis 14:18 - 20*
> *18 - <u>And Melchizedek king of Salem brought forth bread and wine: and he was the priest of the most high God.</u>*
> *19 - <u>And he blessed him, and said, Blessed be Abram of the most high God, possessor of heaven and earth:</u>*
> *20 - <u>And blessed be the most high God, which hath delivered thine enemies into thy hand. And he gave him tithes of all.</u>*

This King brought forth bread and wine for he was the priest of the most high God. This was Abram's first encounter with the possessor of heaven and earth. Up until this time GOD had promised him the land for an inheritance for an earthly seed. Following this encounter Abram was promised a heavenly seed. Abram had to receive a revelation of God as the possessor of heaven and earth before he could receive a heavenly promise. This Melchizedek blessed him, (faith comes by hearing). Abram had to know that the God that he was following possessed both the natural and the spiritual; that the promise would pertain to both the earthly and the heavenly. That this promised seed would be both flesh and Spirit and have a heavenly priesthood. For this Melchizedek was a priest of the most high God. When we read of the tabernacle of David, we remember that he gave bread, flesh and wine to both women and men at the bringing in of the Ark of the Covenant. The covenant that God gave to David was to his son, his seed. David would provide the flesh that would become the sacrifice.

2Samuel 6:17 – 19
17 - And they brought in the ark of the LORD, and set it in his place, in the midst of the tabernacle that David had pitched for it: and David offered burnt offerings and peace offerings before the LORD.
18 - And as soon as David had made an end of offering burnt offerings and peace offerings, he blessed the people in the name of the LORD of hosts.
19 - And he dealt among all the people, even among the whole multitude of Israel, as well to the women as men, to every one a cake of bread, and a good piece of flesh, and a flagon of wine. So all the people departed every one to his house.

Acts 15:16 – 18
16 - After this I will return, and will build again the tabernacle of David, which is fallen down; and I will build again the ruins thereof, and I will set it up:
17 - That the residue of men might seek after the Lord, and all the Gentiles, upon whom my name is called, saith the Lord, who doeth all these things.
18 - Known unto God are all his works from the beginning of the world.

Psalms 76:2
In Salem also is his tabernacle, and his dwelling place in Zion.

Hebrews 7:1 – 4
1 - For this Melchisedec, king of Salem, priest of the most high God, who met Abraham returning from the slaughter of the kings, and blessed him;
2 - To whom also Abraham gave a tenth part of all; first being by interpretation King of righteousness, and after that also King of Salem, which is, King of peace;
3 - Without father, without mother, without descent, having neither beginning of days, nor end of life; but made like unto the Son of God; abideth a priest continually.
4 - Now consider how great this man was, unto whom even the patriarch Abraham gave the tenth of the spoils.

Abram had to know that this seed of promise would be earthly first, then heavenly. First, that which is natural - then, that which is spiritual. A seed that would bring forth bread and wine - word and spirit. Melchizedek was a likeness of the Son of God - both a King and a Priest. A man who would usher in the covenant of God, a mediator between God and man; the man, Christ Jesus.

> *Psalms 110:4*
> *The LORD hath sworn, and will not repent, Thou art a priest for ever after the order of Melchizedek.*
>
> *Hebrews 5:6*
> *As he saith also in another place, Thou art a priest for ever after the order of Melchisedec.*
>
> *Hebrews 6:20*
> *Whither the forerunner is for us entered, even Jesus, made an high priest for ever after the order of Melchisedec.*
>
> *Hebrews 7:15 - 17*
> *15 - And it is yet far more evident: for that after the similitude of Melchisedec there ariseth another priest,*
> *16 - Who is made, not after the law of a carnal commandment, but after the power of an endless life.*
> *17 - For he testifieth, Thou art a priest for ever after the order of Melchisedec.*
>
> *Hebrews 7:21*
> *(For those priests were made without an oath; but this with an oath by him that said unto him, The Lord sware and will not repent, Thou art a priest for ever after the order of Melchisedec:)*
>
> *Luke 22:19 – 20*
> *19 - And he took bread, and gave thanks, and brake it, and gave unto them, saying, This is my body which is given for you: this do in remembrance of me.*
> *20 - Likewise also the cup after supper, saying, This cup is the new testament in my blood, which is shed for you.*

Following this encounter with the King of righteousness, the king of Sodom spoke to Abram.

> *Genesis 14:21 – 24*
> *21 - <u>And the king of Sodom said unto Abram, Give me the persons, and take the goods to thyself.</u>*
> *22 - <u>And Abram said to the king of Sodom, I have lift up mine hand unto the LORD, the most high God, the possessor of heaven and earth,</u>*
> *23 - That I will not take from a thread even to a shoelatchet, and that I will not take any thing that is thine, lest thou shouldest say, I have made Abram rich:*

24 - Save only that which the young men have eaten, and the portion of the men which went with me, Aner, Eshcol, and Mamre; let them take their portion.

The king of Sodom did not acknowledge Melchizedek because he was King of righteousness and there was no righteousness in the king of Sodom. The Light came into the world and darkness comprehended it not. Abram was counted righteous because he believed God. Abram had come into the presence of the LORD, the most high God, the possessor of heaven and earth, the covenant God. With this revelation he was able to withstand the temptation to be bought out by the wicked king. Abram's perception of the LORD had become greater and he had submitted to this most high God who had given his enemies into his hand. He had defeated four kingdoms with three hundred eighteen men. He had become Abram of the most high God and his seed would possess heaven and earth. We cannot submit to what we do not have revelation of. Melchizedek was the revelation of the royal priesthood of the promised seed. After this encounter the LORD promised Abram a heavenly seed. David operated as a king and a priest under the revelation of Melchizedek. David was a type of this new order of covenant.

Genesis 15:1 – 7
1 - After these things the word of the LORD came unto Abram in a vision, saying, Fear not, Abram: I am thy shield, and thy exceeding great reward.
2 - And Abram said, Lord GOD, what wilt thou give me, seeing I go childless, and the steward of my house is this Eliezer of Damascus?
3 - And Abram said, Behold, to me thou hast given no seed: and, lo, one born in my house is mine heir.
4 - And, behold, the word of the LORD came unto him, saying, This shall not be thine heir; but he that shall come forth out of thine own bowels shall be thine heir.
5 - And he brought him forth abroad, and said, Look now toward heaven, and tell the stars, if thou be able to number them: and he said unto him, So shall thy seed be.
6 - And he believed in the LORD; and he counted it to him for righteousness.
7 - And he said unto him, I am the LORD that brought thee out of Ur of the Chaldees, to give thee this land to inherit it.

The LORD had promised Abram that his seed would be both earthly and heavenly and that his seed would possess the land. The two realms of life would once again combine, and man would once again dwell in the heavens and the earth.

THE EARTHLY SEED

The first covenant that the LORD would make with Abram was with his earthly seed. The first king that God gave to Israel was Saul. He represented the natural seed.

> *Genesis 15:8 – 18*
> *8 - And he said, Lord GOD, whereby shall I know that I shall inherit it?*
> *9 - And he said unto him, Take me an heifer of three years old, and a she goat of three years old, and a ram of three years old, and a turtledove, and a young pigeon.*
> *10 - And he took unto him all these, and divided them in the midst, and laid each piece one against another: but the birds divided he not.*
> *11 - And when the fowls came down upon the carcases, Abram drove them away.*
> *12 - And when the sun was going down, a deep sleep fell upon Abram; and, lo, an horror of great darkness fell upon him.*
> *13 - <u>And he said unto Abram, Know of a surety that thy seed shall be a stranger in a land that is not theirs, and shall serve them; and they shall afflict them four hundred years;</u>*
> *14 - And also that nation, whom they shall serve, will I judge: and afterward shall they come out with great substance.*
> *15 - And thou shalt go to thy fathers in peace; thou shalt be buried in a good old age.*
> *16 - But in the fourth generation they shall come hither again: for the iniquity of the Amorites is not yet full.*
> *17 - And it came to pass, that, when the sun went down, and it was dark, behold a smoking furnace, and a burning lamp that passed between those pieces.*
> *18 - <u>In the same day the LORD made a covenant with Abram, saying, Unto thy seed have I given this land, from the river of Egypt unto the great river, the river Euphrates:</u>*

This would be the fulfillment of the first promise, to make of Abram's seed a great nation.

> *Genesis 12:1 – 2*
> *1 - <u>Now the LORD had said unto Abram, Get thee out of thy country, and from thy kindred, and from thy father's house, unto a land that I will shew thee:</u>*
> *2 - <u>And I will make of thee a great nation, and I will bless thee,</u> and make thy name great; and thou shalt be a blessing:*

The fulfillment of this covenant would come after four hundred years of affliction. Saul was anointed king after four hundred years of judges ruling over Israel.

> *Genesis 17:1 – 7*
> *1 - And when Abram was ninety years old and nine, the LORD appeared to Abram, and said unto him, I am the Almighty God; walk before me, and be thou perfect.*

2 - And I will make my covenant between me and thee, and will multiply thee exceedingly.
3 - And Abram fell on his face: and God talked with him, saying,
4 - As for me, behold, my covenant is with thee, and thou shalt be a father of many nations.
5 - Neither shall thy name any more be called Abram, but thy name shall be Abraham; for a father of many nations have I made thee.
6 - And I will make thee exceeding fruitful, and I will make nations of thee, and kings shall come out of thee.
7 - And I will establish my covenant between me and thee and thy seed after thee in their generations for an everlasting covenant, to be a God unto thee, and to thy seed after thee.

We notice that in these scriptures that the LORD told Abram that He will make his covenant with him. He then said, "My covenant is with thee". This is the promise of the second part of the covenant with Abram. The first part was made with Abram concerning his earthly seed.

Genesis 15:18
In the same day the LORD made a covenant with Abram, saying, Unto thy seed have I given this land, from the river of Egypt unto the great river, the river Euphrates.

The second part would be with his heavenly seed for an everlasting covenant. I stated earlier Abram's covenant would be a two-fold covenant.

THE HEAVENLY SEED

Genesis 17:7
And I will establish my covenant between me and thee and thy seed after thee in their generations for an everlasting covenant, to be a God unto thee, and to thy seed after thee.

The first part of the covenant pertained to a nation the second pertained to many nations.

Genesis 12:1 – 2
1 - Now the LORD had said unto Abram, Get thee out of thy country, and from thy kindred, and from thy father's house, unto a land that I will shew thee:
2 - And I will make of thee a great nation, and I will bless thee, and make thy name great; and thou shalt be a blessing:

Gen 17:4 – 5
4 - As for me, behold, my covenant is with thee, and thou shalt be a father of many nations.
5 - Neither shall thy name any more be called Abram, but thy name shall be Abraham; for a father of many nations have I made thee.

THE TWO-FOLD PROMISE

This two-fold covenant would be established with Isaac and Jacob.

> *Exodus 2:24*
> *And God heard their groaning, and God remembered <u>his covenant with Abraham, with Isaac, and with Jacob</u>.*

This scripture says covenant singular, this indicates that this is one covenant established with all three of these men. Isaac was the son of promise and Jacob was his son. Abraham's two-fold covenant would be established through Isaac and Jacob.

> *Genesis 26:1 – 5*
> *1 - And there was a famine in the land, beside the first famine that was in the days of Abraham. And Isaac went unto Abimelech king of the Philistines unto Gerar.*
> *2 - And <u>the LORD</u> appeared unto him, and said, Go not down into Egypt; dwell in the land which I shall tell thee of:*
> *3 - Sojourn in this land, and I will be with thee, and will bless thee; for unto thee, and unto thy seed, I will give all these countries, <u>and I will perform the oath which I sware unto Abraham thy father;</u>*
> *4 - And I will make thy seed to multiply as the stars of heaven, and will give unto thy seed all these countries; <u>and in thy seed shall all the nations of the earth be blessed;</u>*
> *5 - <u>because that Abraham obeyed my voice, and kept my charge, my commandments, my statutes, and my laws.</u>*

> *Genesis 28:10 – 17*
> *10 - And Jacob went out from Beersheba, and went toward Haran.*
> *11 - And he lighted upon a certain place, and tarried there all night, because the sun was set; and he took of the stones of that place, and put them for his pillows, and lay down in that place to sleep.*
> *12 - And he dreamed, and behold a ladder set up on the earth, and the top of it reached to heaven: and behold the angels of God ascending and descending on it.*
> *13 - And, behold, the LORD stood above it, and said<u>, I am the LORD God of Abraham thy father, and the God of Isaac: the land whereon thou liest, to thee will I give it, and to thy seed;</u>*
> *14 - And thy seed shall be as the dust of the earth, and thou shalt spread abroad to the west, and to the east, and to the north, and to the south: and in thee and in thy seed shall all the families of the earth be blessed.*
> *15 - And, behold, I am with thee, and will keep thee in all places whither thou goest, and will bring thee again into this land; for I will not leave thee, until I have done that which I have spoken to thee of.*
> *16 - And Jacob awaked out of his sleep, and he said, <u>Surely the LORD is in this place;</u> and I knew it not.*
> *17 - And he was afraid, and said, How dreadful is this place! this is none other but the house of God, and this is the gate of heaven.*

In verse 13 we read that when referring to Abraham, He is LORD God and with Isaac he is God. This confirms that the covenant was made with Abraham and will be established with Isaac and Jacob. When talking to Isaac the LORD spoke of the stars of heaven (heavenly seed) and to Jacob the dust of the earth (earthly seed). This confirms that the promise was first given by faith.

> *Galatians 3:6 – 8, 16 – 18*
> *6 - Even as Abraham believed God, and it was accounted to him for righteousness.*
> *7 - <u>Know ye therefore that they which are of faith, the same are the children of Abraham.</u>*
> *8 - And the scripture, foreseeing that God would justify the heathen through faith, preached before the gospel unto Abraham, saying, In thee shall all nations be blessed.*
>
> *16 - Now to Abraham and his seed were the promises made. He saith not, and to seeds, as of many; but as of one, And to thy seed, which is Christ.*
> *17 - And this I say, that the covenant, that was confirmed before of God in Christ, <u>the law, which was four hundred and thirty years after</u>, cannot disannul, that it should make the promise of none effect.*
> *18 - <u>For if the inheritance be of the law, it is no more of promise: but God gave it to Abraham by promise.</u>*

These scriptures confirm that the first covenant to be instituted would be the covenant of law. This covenant would be brought forth through Jacob. The second covenant would be the covenant of faith. We read that King Saul only operated under the law, yet King David operated outside of the law.

> *Galatians 3:11*
> *But that no man is justified by the law in the sight of God, it is evident: for, <u>The just shall live by faith.</u>*

These two covenants would fulfill the covenant that the LORD God made with Abraham.

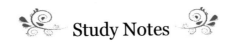

Chapter 6

The Covenant of Law

Genesis 2:14
And the name of the third river is Hiddekel: that is it which goeth toward the east of Assyria.

The third river head is Hiddekel which means rapid or quick work. This is a river head coming out of Eden. In previous chapters we have searched the scriptures and found that these river heads are covenants that would flow out of Eden to man. The first river Pison (dispersive) was a covenant established with Noah between The LORD God and the earth. The second river Gihon (bursting forth) was the two-fold covenant that the LORD God made with Abraham that would cover the whole earth, land and nations. The third river head would be the first part of the promise given to the serpent and to Abraham. As we look back at Eve we see that Cain was a type of the covenant with the earth and he was a type of un-regenerated man or wicked seed. We will now look at Abel, the second son of Eve.

Genesis 3:15
And I will put enmity between thee and the woman, and between thy seed and her seed<u>; it shall bruise thy head</u>, and thou shalt bruise his heel.

Genesis 4:1 – 2
1 - And Adam knew Eve his wife; and she conceived, and bare Cain, and said, I have gotten a man from the LORD.
2 - <u>And she again bare his brother Abel. And Abel was a keeper of sheep</u>, but Cain was a tiller of the ground.

KEEPER OF SHEEP

Notice that Abel was a keeper of sheep. When we search the scriptures, we find that Moses was the first mentioned keeper of sheep. Abram had sheep, but Moses was a keeper of sheep.

Exodus 3:1
<u>Now Moses kept the flock of Jethro his father in law</u>, the priest of Midian: and he led the flock to the backside of the desert, and came to the mountain of God, even to Horeb.

Moses would bring forth the covenant that the LORD had promised Abraham concerning his earthly seed, fulfilling the prophecy of the four hundred years of affliction.

Exodus 3:2 – 8

2 - And the angel of the LORD appeared unto him in a flame of fire out of the midst of a bush: and he looked, and, behold, the bush burned with fire, and the bush was not consumed.

3 - And Moses said, I will now turn aside, and see this great sight, why the bush is not burnt.

4 - And when the LORD saw that he turned aside to see, God called unto him out of the midst of the bush, and said, Moses, Moses. And he said, Here am I.

5 - And he said, Draw not nigh hither: put off thy shoes from off thy feet, for the place whereon thou standest is holy ground.

6 - Moreover he said, <u>I am the God of thy father, the God of Abraham, the God of Isaac, and the God of Jacob.</u> And Moses hid his face; for he was afraid to look upon God.

7 - <u>And the LORD said, I have surely seen the affliction of my people which are in Egypt, and have heard their cry by reason of their taskmasters; for I know their sorrows;</u>

8 - <u>And I am come down to deliver them out of the hand of the Egyptians, and to bring them up out of that land unto a good land and a large, unto a land flowing with milk and honey; unto the place of the Canaanites, and the Hittites, and the Amorites, and the Perizzites, and the Hivites, and the Jebusites.</u>

Genesis 15:8 – 18

8 - And he said, Lord GOD, whereby shall I know that I shall inherit it?

9 - And he said unto him, Take me an heifer of three years old, and a she goat of three years old, and a ram of three years old, and a turtledove, and a young pigeon.

10 - And he took unto him all these, and divided them in the midst, and laid each piece one against another: but the birds divided he not.

11 - And when the fowls came down upon the carcases, Abram drove them away.

12 - And when the sun was going down, a deep sleep fell upon Abram; and, lo, an horror of great darkness fell upon him.

13 - <u>And he said unto Abram, Know of a surety that thy seed shall be a stranger in a land that is not theirs, and shall serve them; and they shall afflict them four hundred years;</u>

14 - <u>And also that nation, whom they shall serve, will I judge: and afterward shall they come out with great substance.</u>

15 - And thou shalt go to thy fathers in peace; thou shalt be buried in a good old age.

16 - But in the fourth generation they shall come hither again: for the iniquity of the Amorites is not yet full.

17 - And it came to pass, that, when the sun went down, and it was dark, behold a smoking furnace, and a burning lamp that passed between those pieces.

18 - <u>In the same day the LORD made a covenant with Abram, saying, Unto thy seed have I given this land, from the river of Egypt unto the great river, the river Euphrates:</u>

The promise that was given to Jacob extended from Abram, a promise that would bless the families of the earth.

> *Genesis 28:10 – 17*
> *10 - And Jacob went out from Beersheba, and went toward Haran.*
> *11 - And he lighted upon a certain place, and tarried there all night, because the sun was set; and he took of the stones of that place, and put them for his pillows, and lay down in that place to sleep.*
> *12 - And he dreamed, and behold a ladder set up on the earth, and the top of it reached to heaven: and behold the angels of God ascending and descending on it.*
> *13 - <u>And, behold, the LORD stood above it, and said, I am the LORD God of Abraham thy father, and the God of Isaac: the land whereon thou liest, to thee will I give it, and to thy seed;</u>*
> *14 - <u>And thy seed shall be as the dust of the earth, and thou shalt spread abroad to the west, and to the east, and to the north, and to the south: and in thee and in thy seed shall all the families of the earth be blessed.</u>*
> *15 - And, behold, I am with thee, and will keep thee in all places whither thou goest, and will bring thee again into this land; for I will not leave thee, until I have done that which I have spoken to thee of.*
> *16 - And Jacob awaked out of his sleep, and he said, Surely the LORD is in this place; and I knew it not.*
> *17 - And he was afraid, and said, How dreadful is this place! this is none other but the house of God, and this is the gate of heaven.*

Notice in verse thirteen that he is LORD God of Abraham and he refers to Abraham as Jacob's father. This signifies that the covenant is with Abraham and that he is father to all who are under this covenant. In verse 16 Jacob recognized him as LORD.

A PROPHECY FUFILLED

Jacob and his sons would go into the land of Egypt.

> *Psalms 105:23 – 37*
> *23 - <u>Israel also came into Egypt; and Jacob sojourned in the land of Ham.</u>*
> *24 - And he increased his people greatly; and made them stronger than their enemies.*
> *25 - He turned their heart to hate his people, to deal subtilly with his servants.*
> *26 - He sent Moses his servant; and Aaron whom he had chosen.*
> *27 - They shewed his signs among them, and wonders in the land of Ham.*
> *28 - He sent darkness, and made it dark; and they rebelled not against his word.*
> *29 - He turned their waters into blood, and slew their fish.*
> *30 - Their land brought forth frogs in abundance, in the chambers of their kings.*
> *31 - He spake, and there came divers sorts of flies, and lice in all their coasts.*

32 - He gave them hail for rain, and flaming fire in their land.
33 - He smote their vines also and their fig trees; and brake the trees of their coasts.
34 - He spake, and the locusts came, and caterpillers, and that without number,
35 - And did eat up all the herbs in their land, and devoured the fruit of their ground.
36 - He smote also all the firstborn in their land, the chief of all their strength.
37 - He brought them forth also with silver and gold: and there was not one feeble person among their tribes.

The LORD would remember his covenant with Abraham.

Psalms 105:42 – 43
42 - <u>For he remembered his holy promise, and Abraham his servant.</u>
43 - And he brought forth his people with joy, and his chosen with gladness:

This covenant would be made after the four hundred years of bondage. It was made with Moses and with Israel. It was made on the mercy seat between the two Cherubim. The Cherubim were set east of the garden to keep the way of the tree of life.

Exodus 20:1 – 17
1 - And God spake all these words, saying,
2 - <u>I am the LORD thy God</u>, which have brought thee out of the land of Egypt, out of the house of bondage.
3 - Thou shalt have no other gods before me.
4 - Thou shalt not make unto thee any graven image, or any likeness of any thing that is in heaven above, or that is in the earth beneath, or that is in the water under the earth:
5 - Thou shalt not bow down thyself to them, nor serve them: for I the LORD thy God am a jealous God, visiting the iniquity of the fathers upon the children unto the third and fourth generation of them that hate me;
6 - And shewing mercy unto thousands of them that love me, and keep my commandments.
7 - Thou shalt not take the name of the LORD thy God in vain; for the LORD will not hold him guiltless that taketh his name in vain.
8 - Remember the sabbath day, to keep it holy.
9 - Six days shalt thou labour, and do all thy work:
10 - But the seventh day is the sabbath of the LORD thy God: in it thou shalt not do any work, thou, nor thy son, nor thy daughter, thy manservant, nor thy maidservant, nor thy cattle, nor thy stranger that is within thy gates:
11 - For in six days the LORD made heaven and earth, the sea, and all that in them is, and rested the seventh day: wherefore the LORD blessed the sabbath day, and hallowed it.
12 - Honour thy father and thy mother: that thy days may be long upon the land which the LORD thy God giveth thee.
13 - Thou shalt not kill.
14 - Thou shalt not commit adultery.
15 - Thou shalt not steal.

16 - Thou shalt not bear false witness against thy neighbour.
17 - Thou shalt not covet thy neighbour's house, thou shalt not covet thy neighbour's wife, nor his manservant, nor his maidservant, nor his ox, nor his ass, nor any thing that is thy neighbour's.

Exodus 25:17 – 22
17 - And thou shalt make a mercy seat of pure gold: two cubits and a half shall be the length thereof, and a cubit and a half the breadth thereof.
18 - And thou shalt make two <u>cherubims</u> of gold, of beaten work shalt thou make them<u>, in the two ends of the mercy seat.</u>
19 - And make one cherub on the one end, and the other cherub on the other end: even of the mercy seat shall ye make the cherubims on the two ends thereof.
20 - <u>And the cherubims shall stretch forth their wings on high, covering the mercy seat with their wings, and their faces shall look one to another; toward the mercy seat shall the faces of the cherubims be.</u>
21 - <u>And thou shalt put the mercy seat above upon the ark; and in the ark thou shalt put the testimony that I shall give thee.</u>
22 - <u>And there I will meet with thee, and I will commune with thee from above the mercy seat, from between the two cherubims which are upon the ark of the testimony, of all things which I will give thee in commandment unto the children of Israel.</u>

Exodus 34:27 – 28
27 - And the LORD said unto Moses, <u>Write thou these words: for after the tenor of these words I have made a covenant with thee and with Israel.</u>
28 - And he was there with the LORD forty days and forty nights; he did neither eat bread, nor drink water. <u>And he wrote upon the tables the words of the covenant, the ten commandments.</u>

<u>A BLOOD COVENANT</u>

This covenant was confirmed with blood. This was a written covenant. The first part of the promise that God made with the serpent in the garden. The written word of God.

Genesis 3:15
And I will put enmity between thee and the woman, and between thy seed and her seed<u>; it shall bruise thy head</u>, and thou shalt bruise his heel.

Exodus 24:1 – 8
1 - And he said unto Moses, Come up unto the LORD, thou, and Aaron, Nadab, and Abihu, and seventy of the elders of Israel; and worship ye afar off.
2 - And Moses alone shall come near the LORD: but they shall not come nigh; neither shall the people go up with him.
3 - And Moses came and told the people all the words of the LORD, and all the judgments: and all the people answered with one voice, and said, All the words which the LORD hath said will we do.

4 - <u>And Moses wrote all the words of the LORD, and rose up early in the morning, and builded an altar under the hill, and twelve pillars, according to the twelve tribes of Israel.</u>
5 - <u>And he sent young men of the children of Israel, which offered burnt offerings, and sacrificed peace offerings of oxen unto the LORD.</u>
6 - <u>And Moses took half of the blood, and put it in basons; and half of the blood he sprinkled on the altar.</u>
7 - <u>And he took the book of the covenant, and read in the audience of the people: and they said, All that the LORD hath said will we do, and be obedient.</u>
8 - <u>And Moses took the blood, and sprinkled it on the people, and said, Behold the blood of the covenant, which the LORD hath made with you concerning all these words.</u>

Hebrews 9:18 – 22
18 - <u>Whereupon neither the first testament was dedicated without blood.</u>
19 - <u>For when Moses had spoken every precept to all the people according to the law, he took the blood of calves and of goats, with water, and scarlet wool, and hyssop, and sprinkled both the book, and all the people,</u>
20 - <u>Saying, This is the blood of the testament which God hath enjoined unto you.</u>
21 - <u>Moreover he sprinkled with blood both the tabernacle, and all the vessels of the ministry.</u>
22 - <u>And almost all things are by the law purged with blood; and without shedding of blood is no remission.</u>

When we look at the covenant of law we can see the type of Abel. He was a keeper of sheep and as we searched the scriptures we found that Moses was a keeper of sheep.

Genesis 4:3 – 4
3 – And in process of time it came to pass, that Cain brought of the fruit of the ground an offering unto the LORD.
4 - <u>And Abel, he also brought of the firstlings of his flock and of the fat thereof. And the LORD had respect unto Abel and to his offering:</u>

Abel was a keeper of sheep and brought the firstlings of his flock. We see this in comparison with Israel at the Passover. Abel's sacrifice was accepted as was the sacrifice of Israel of the Passover lamb.

Exodus 12:3 – 14, 21 – 27
3 - Speak ye unto all the congregation of Israel, <u>saying, In the tenth day of this month they shall take to them every man a lamb,</u> according to the house of their fathers, a lamb for an house:
4 - And if the household be too little for the lamb, let him and his neighbour next unto his house take it according to the number of the souls; every man according to his eating shall make your count for the lamb.
5 - Your lamb shall be without blemish, a male of the first year: ye shall take it out from the sheep, or from the goats:
6 - And ye shall keep it up until the fourteenth day of the same month: and the whole assembly of the congregation of Israel shall kill it in the evening.

7 - And they shall take of the blood, and strike it on the two side posts and on the upper door post of the houses, wherein they shall eat it.

8 - And they shall eat the flesh in that night, roast with fire, and unleavened bread; and with bitter herbs they shall eat it.

9 - Eat not of it raw, nor sodden at all with water, but roast with fire; his head with his legs, and with the purtenance thereof.

10 - And ye shall let nothing of it remain until the morning; and that which remaineth of it until the morning ye shall burn with fire.

11 - And thus shall ye eat it; with your loins girded, your shoes on your feet, and your staff in your hand; and ye shall eat it in haste: it is the LORD'S passover.

12 - For I will pass through the land of Egypt this night, and will smite all the firstborn in the land of Egypt, both man and beast; and against all the gods of Egypt I will execute judgment: I am the LORD.

13 - And the blood shall be to you for a token upon the houses where ye are: and when I see the blood, I will pass over you, and the plague shall not be upon you to destroy you, when I smite the land of Egypt.

14 - And this day shall be unto you for a memorial; and ye shall keep it a feast to the LORD throughout your generations; ye shall keep it a feast by an ordinance for ever.

21 - Then Moses called for all the elders of Israel, and said unto them, Draw out and take you a lamb according to your families, and kill the passover.

22 - And ye shall take a bunch of hyssop, and dip it in the blood that is in the bason, and strike the lintel and the two side posts with the blood that is in the bason; and none of you shall go out at the door of his house until the morning.

23 - For the LORD will pass through to smite the Egyptians; and when he seeth the blood upon the lintel, and on the two side posts, the LORD will pass over the door, and will not suffer the destroyer to come in unto your houses to smite you.

24 - And ye shall observe this thing for an ordinance to thee and to thy sons for ever.

25 - And it shall come to pass, when ye be come to the land which the LORD will give you, according as he hath promised, that ye shall keep this service.

26 - And it shall come to pass, when your children shall say unto you, What mean ye by this service?

27 - That ye shall say, It is the sacrifice of the LORD'S passover, who passed over the houses of the children of Israel in Egypt, when he smote the Egyptians, and delivered our houses. And the people bowed the head and worshipped.

The writer referring to Abel's sacrifice when ministering to the Hebrews about the new and better covenant. Making distinction between Mount Sinai and Mount Sion, the old and the new covenants. Stating that on Mount Sinai His voice shook the earth but on Mount Sion, he shakes both the earth and heaven.

Hebrews 12:18 – 29
18 - <u>For ye are not come unto the mount that might be touched, and that burned with fire, nor unto blackness, and darkness, and tempest,</u>

19 - And the sound of a trumpet, and the voice of words; which voice they that heard intreated that the word should not be spoken to them any more:
20 - (For they could not endure that which was commanded, And if so much as a beast touch the mountain, it shall be stoned, or thrust through with a dart:
21 - And so terrible was the sight, that Moses said, I exceedingly fear and quake:)
22 - But ye are come unto mount Sion, and unto the city of the living God, the heavenly Jerusalem, and to an innumerable company of angels,
23 - To the general assembly and church of the firstborn, which are written in heaven, and to God the Judge of all, and to the spirits of just men made perfect,
24 - And to Jesus the mediator of the new covenant, and to the blood of sprinkling, that speaketh better things than that of Abel.
25 - See that ye refuse not him that speaketh. For if they escaped not who refused him that spake on earth, much more shall not we escape, if we turn away from him that speaketh from heaven:
26 - Whose voice then shook the earth: but now he hath promised, saying, Yet once more I shake not the earth only, but also heaven.
27 - And this word, Yet once more, signifieth the removing of those things that are shaken, as of things that are made, that those things which cannot be shaken may remain.
28 - Wherefore we receiving a kingdom which cannot be moved, let us have grace, whereby we may serve God acceptably with reverence and godly fear:
29 - For our God is a consuming fire.

They refused him that spoke on the earth. Scripture warns the Hebrews not to refuse the one who continues to speak from heaven.

Exodus 20:18 – 19
18 - And all the people saw the thunderings, and the lightnings, and the noise of the trumpet, and the mountain smoking: and when the people saw it, they removed, and stood afar off.
19 - And they said unto Moses, Speak thou with us, and we will hear: but let not God speak with us, lest we die.

Hebrews 12:18 – 21
18 - For ye are not come unto the mount that might be touched, and that burned with fire, nor unto blackness, and darkness, and tempest,
19 - And the sound of a trumpet, and the voice of words; which voice they that heard intreated that the word should not be spoken to them any more:
20 - (For they could not endure that which was commanded, And if so much as a beast touch the mountain, it shall be stoned, or thrust through with a dart:
21 - And so terrible was the sight, that Moses said, I exceedingly fear and quake:)

Hebrews compared the sacrifice of Abel to the sacrifice of the Old Testament that would Be done away with. The writer also stated that these are two covenants, one on Mount Sinai and the other, Jerusalem (Mount Sion). King Saul would rule under the law of Mount Sinai but King David would rule in Mount Sion.

> *Hebrews 12:22 – 24*
> *22 - <u>But ye are come unto mount Sion, and unto the city of the living God, the heavenly Jerusalem, and to an innumerable company of angels,</u>*
> *23 - To the general assembly and church of the firstborn, which are written in heaven, and to God the Judge of all, and to the spirits of just men made perfect,*
> *24 - <u>And to Jesus the mediator of the new covenant, and to the blood of sprinkling, that speaketh better things than that of Abel.</u>*
>
> *Galatians 4:21 – 31*
> *21 - Tell me, ye that desire to be under the law, do ye not hear the law?*
> *22 - For it is written, that Abraham had two sons, the one by a bondmaid, the other by a freewoman.*
> *23 - But he who was of the bondwoman was born after the flesh; but he of the freewoman was by promise.*
> *24 - Which things are an allegory: <u>for these are the two covenants; the one from the mount Sinai, which gendereth to bondage, which is Agar.</u>*
> *25 - For this Agar is mount Sinai in Arabia, and answereth to Jerusalem which now is, and is in bondage with her children.*
> *26 - <u>But Jerusalem which is above is free, which is the mother of us all.</u>*
> *27 - For it is written, Rejoice, thou barren that bearest not; break forth and cry, thou that travailest not: for the desolate hath many more children than she which hath an husband.*
> *28 - <u>Now we, brethren, as Isaac was, are the children of promise.</u>*
> *29 - But as then he that was born after the flesh persecuted him that was born after the Spirit, even so it is now.*
> *30 - <u>Nevertheless what saith the scripture? Cast out the bondwoman and her son: for the son of the bondwoman shall not be heir with the son of the freewoman.</u>*
> *31 - <u>So then, brethren, we are not children of the bondwoman, but of the free.</u>*

THE OLD AND THE NEW

A new covenant would come forth to replace the old. When we look at the sons of Eve, we see that a new seed would be born to replace the one who was slain.

> *Genesis 4:25*
> *And Adam knew his wife again; and she bare a son, <u>and called his name Seth: For God, said she, hath appointed me another seed instead of Abel, whom Cain slew.</u>*

When Eve bare Cain she said that she had gotten a man from the LORD. In chapter four we searched out the scriptures and found Cain to be a type of the covenant with Noah and a type of the un-regenerated man. The wicked who would be cursed from the earth. Here we read that Eve bare another son and said God had appointed another seed instead of Abel. By this we know that Eve knew that Abel was the first seed. The type of the first of the two-fold covenant that God would make with man. Jesus compared the wicked men of His day to Cain and the prophets and the righteous to Abel.

Matthew 23:29 – 35
29 - Woe unto you, scribes and Pharisees, hypocrites! because ye build the tombs of the prophets, and garnish the sepulchres of the righteous,
30 - And say, If we had been in the days of our fathers, we would not have been partakers with them in the blood of the prophets.
31 - Wherefore ye be witnesses unto yourselves, that ye are the children of them which killed the prophets.
32 - Fill ye up then the measure of your fathers.
33 - Ye serpents, ye generation of vipers, how can ye escape the damnation of hell?
34 - Wherefore, behold, I send unto you prophets, and wise men, and scribes: and some of them ye shall kill and crucify; and some of them shall ye scourge in your synagogues, and persecute them from city to city:
35 - That upon you may come all the righteous blood shed upon the earth, from the blood of righteous Abel unto the blood of Zacharias son of Barachias, whom ye slew between the temple and the altar.

Matthew 27:25 – 26
25 - Then answered all the people, and said, His blood be on us, and on our children.
26 - Then released he Barabbas unto them: and when he had scourged Jesus, he delivered him to be crucified.

This wicked generation would slay Jesus on the cross doing away with the old covenant and establishing the new. Just as Cain slew Abel and was replaced by Seth the appointed seed.

Colossians 2:14
Blotting out the handwriting of ordinances that was against us, which was contrary to us, and took it out of the way, nailing it to his cross;

Hebrews 9:1
Then verily the first covenant had also ordinances of divine service, and a worldly sanctuary.

Hebrews 9:15 - 17
15 - And for this cause he is the mediator of the new testament, that by means of death, for the redemption of the transgressions that were under the first testament, they which are called might receive the promise of eternal inheritance.
16 - For where a testament is, there must also of necessity be the death of the testator.

17 - <u>For a testament is of force after men are dead: otherwise it is of no strength at all while the testator liveth.</u>

Jesus did not come to destroy the law or the prophets but to destroy the works of the devil.

Matthew 5:17 – 18
17 - <u>Think not that I am come to destroy the law, or the prophets: I am not come to destroy, but to fulfil.</u>
18 - For verily I say unto you, Till heaven and earth pass, one jot or one tittle shall in no wise pass from the law, till all be fulfilled.

1John 3:8
He that committeth sin is of the devil; for the devil sinneth from the beginning. For this purpose the Son of God was manifested, <u>that he might destroy the works of the devil.</u>

We conclude this chapter with the bringing in of another seed.

Genesis 4:25
And Adam knew his wife again; and she bare a son, <u>and called his name Seth: For God, said she hath appointed me another seed instead of Abel, whom Cain slew.</u>

Chapter 7

The Covenant of Faith

Genesis 2:14
And the name of the third river is Hiddekel: that is it which goeth toward the east of Assyria. <u>And the fourth river is Euphrates.</u>

Euphrates is the fourth and final river head coming out of the Garden of Eden. Euphrates means prosperity, fruitfulness or breaking forth. This is the second and final covenant that God had promised to the serpent and Abraham.

Genesis 3:15
And I will put enmity between thee and the woman, <u>and between thy seed and her seed; it shall bruise thy head, and thou shalt bruise his heel.</u>

Genesis 22:15 – 18
15 - And the angel of the LORD called unto Abraham out of heaven the second time,
16 - And said, By myself have I sworn, saith the LORD, for because thou hast done this thing, and hast not withheld thy son, thine only son:
17 - That in blessing I will bless thee, <u>and in multiplying I will multiply thy seed as the stars of the heaven, and as the sand which is upon the sea shore; and thy seed shall possess the gate of his enemies;</u>
18 - <u>And in thy seed shall all the nations of the earth be blessed; because thou hast obeyed my voice.</u>

Galatians 3:6 – 9, 16
6 - <u>Even as Abraham believed God, and it was accounted to him for righteousness.</u>
7 - <u>Know ye therefore that they which are of faith, the same are the children of Abraham.</u>
8 - <u>And the scripture, foreseeing that God would justify the heathen through faith, preached before the gospel unto Abraham, saying, In thee shall all nations be blessed.</u>
9 - <u>So then they which be of faith are blessed with faithful Abraham.</u>

16 - Now to Abraham and his seed were the promises made. <u>He saith not, And to seeds, as of many; but as of one, And to thy seed, which is Christ.</u>

THE FLAMING SWORD

This covenant is the flaming sword that keeps the way to the tree of life. We studied in previous chapters that God placed the Cherubims and the flaming sword to keep the way, and that these represent the two covenants that would come out of Eden to bring man, back to the tree of life. The written word was given to Moses out of the midst of the mercy seat between the Cherubims.

The flaming sword is:
- the sword of the Spirit which is the word of God,
- the word made flesh,
- the seed which is Christ,
- the Rhema word that lives in the believers,
- the bread of God and
- the water of life.

Ephesians 6:17
And take the helmet of salvation, and the sword of the Spirit, which is the word of God:

Hebrews 4:12
For the word of God is quick, and powerful, and sharper than any twoedged sword, piercing even to the dividing asunder of soul and spirit, and of the joints and marrow, and is a discerner of the thoughts and intents of the heart.

Revelation 1:16
And he had in his right hand seven stars: and out of his mouth went a sharp twoedged sword: and his countenance was as the sun shineth in his strength.

Revelation 2:12
And to the angel of the church in Pergamos write; These things saith he which hath the sharp sword with two edges;

The word of God is a two-edged sword, just as the promise God gave to the serpent, one side to bring judgement and the other to bring redemption.

Matthew 4:4
But he answered and said, It is written, Man shall not live by bread alone, but by every word that proceedeth out of the mouth of God.

John 6:32 – 35
32 - Then Jesus said unto them, Verily, verily, I say unto you, Moses gave you not that bread from heaven; but my Father giveth you the true bread from heaven.
33 - For the bread of God is he which cometh down from heaven, and giveth life unto the world.
34 - Then said they unto him, Lord, evermore give us this bread.
35 - And Jesus said unto them, I am the bread of life: he that cometh to me shall never hunger; and he that believeth on me shall never thirst.

John 7:37 – 38
37 - In the last day, that great day of the feast, Jesus stood and cried, saying, If any man thirst, let him come unto me, and drink.
38 - He that believeth on me, as the scripture hath said, out of his belly shall flow rivers of living water.

Genesis 3:15
And I will put enmity between thee and the woman, and between thy seed and her seed; it shall bruise thy head, <u>and thou shalt bruise his heel.</u>

Isaiah 53:3 – 12
3 - He is despised and rejected of men; a man of sorrows, and acquainted with grief: and we hid as it were our faces from him; he was despised, and we esteemed him not.
4 - Surely he hath borne our griefs, and carried our sorrows: yet we did esteem him stricken, smitten of God, and afflicted.
5 - But he was wounded for our transgressions, <u>he was bruised for our iniquities:</u> the chastisement of our peace was upon him; and with his stripes we are healed.
6 - All we like sheep have gone astray; we have turned every one to his own way; and the LORD hath laid on him the iniquity of us all.
7 - He was oppressed, and he was afflicted, yet he opened not his mouth: <u>he is brought as a lamb to the slaughter</u>, and as a sheep before her shearers is dumb, so he openeth not his mouth.
8 - He was taken from prison and from judgment: and who shall declare his generation? For he was cut off out of the land of the living: for the transgression of my people was he stricken.
9 - And he made his grave with the wicked, and with the rich in his death; because he had done no violence, neither was any deceit in his mouth.
10 - <u>Yet it pleased the LORD to bruise him; he hath put him to grief: when thou shalt make his soul an offering for sin, he shall see his seed, he shall prolong his days, and the pleasure of the LORD shall prosper in his hand.</u>
11 - He shall see of the travail of his soul, and shall be satisfied: by his knowledge shall my righteous servant justify many; for he shall bear their iniquities.
12 - Therefore will I divide him a portion with the great, and he shall divide the spoil with the strong; because he hath poured out his soul unto death: and he was numbered with the transgressors; and he bare the sin of many, and made intercession for the transgressors.

This is the final covenant that God would make with man. A covenant that would open the way to the tree of life and bring man back to the garden. The Paradise of God where they may eat of the tree of life.

John 14:6
Jesus saith unto him<u>, I am the way,</u> the truth, and the life: no man cometh unto the Father, but by me.

Revelation 2:7
He that hath an ear, let him hear what <u>the Spirit saith unto the churches;</u> To him that overcometh <u>will I give to eat of the tree of life, which is in the midst of the paradise of God.</u>

SETH, AN APPOINTED SEED

Chapter six ended with the third son of Eve. We will search out the scriptures comparing this third son with the final covenant that would be given to man.

> *Genesis 4:25*
> *And Adam knew his wife again; <u>and she bare a son, and called his name Seth: For God, said she, hath appointed me another seed instead of Abel, whom Cain slew.</u>*

Eve called his name Seth which means appointed. She knew that he would bring forth the seed that would conquer the enemy and bring man back to God.

> *Genesis 4:26*
> *<u>And to Seth, to him also there was born a son; and he called his name Enos: then began men to call upon the name of the LORD.</u>*

This scripture states that to Seth was born a son that would bring man back to covenant with God (LORD). That he would bring man the name of the LORD.

> *Genesis 5:3*
> *And Adam lived an hundred and thirty years, <u>and begat a son in his own likeness,</u> after his image; and called his name Seth:*

THE LIKENESS OF ADAM

Seth would be born in the likeness of Adam, in his image. Since we know that this son is a type of the covenant that would be given to man, let us search the word. The next covenant the LORD makes will be with King David.

> *1Chronicles 17:2 – 15*
> *2 - Then Nathan said unto David, Do all that is in thine heart; for God is with thee.*
> *3 - And it came to pass the same night, that the word of God came to Nathan, saying,*
> *4 - <u>Go and tell David my servant, Thus saith the LORD, Thou shalt not build me an house to dwell in:</u>*
> *5 - For I have not dwelt in an house since the day that I brought up Israel unto this day; but have gone from tent to tent, and from one tabernacle to another.*
> *6 - Wheresoever I have walked with all Israel, spake I a word to any of the judges of Israel, whom I commanded to feed my people, saying, Why have ye not built me an house of cedars?*
> *7 - Now therefore thus shalt thou say unto my servant David, Thus saith the LORD of hosts, I took thee from the sheepcote, even from following the sheep, that thou shouldest be ruler over my people Israel:*

8 - And I have been with thee whithersoever thou hast walked, and have cut off all thine enemies from before thee, and have made thee a name like the name of the great men that are in the earth.
9 - Also I will ordain a place for my people Israel, and will plant them, and they shall dwell in their place, and shall be moved no more; neither shall the children of wickedness waste them any more, as at the beginning,
10 - And since the time that I commanded judges to be over my people Israel. Moreover I will subdue all thine enemies. <u>Furthermore I tell thee that the LORD will build thee an house.</u>
11 - <u>And it shall come to pass, when thy days be expired that thou must go to be with thy fathers, that I will raise up thy seed after thee, which shall be of thy sons; and I will establish his kingdom.</u>
12 - <u>He shall build me an house, and I will stablish his throne for ever.</u>
13 - <u>I will be his father, and he shall be my son: and I will not take my mercy away from him, as I took it from him that was before thee:</u>
14 - <u>But I will settle him in mine house and in my kingdom for ever: and his throne shall be established for evermore.</u>
15 - According to all these words, and according to all this vision, so did Nathan speak unto David.

2Chronicles 21:7
Howbeit the LORD would not destroy the house of David, <u>because of the covenant that he had made with David, and as he promised to give a light to him and to his sons for ever.</u>

The LORD made covenant with David that out of his sons would come a seed that would have an everlasting kingdom. David was king of Judah; his seed would come out of Judah.

John 7:42
Hath not the scripture said, <u>That Christ cometh of the seed of David,</u> and out of the town of Bethlehem, where David was?

Hebrews 7:13 - 14
13 - For he of whom these things are spoken pertaineth to another tribe, of which no man gave attendance at the altar.
14 - <u>For it is evident that our Lord sprang out of Juda; of which tribe Moses spake nothing concerning priesthood.</u>

David was born in the likeness of Adam.

Genesis 5:3
And Adam lived an hundred and thirty years, <u>and begat a son in his own likeness;</u>

Psalms 51:5
<u>Behold, I was shapen in iniquity; and in sin did my mother conceive me.</u>

David's son would be born in his likeness.

> *Romans 8:3*
> *For what the law could not do, in that it was weak through the flesh, <u>God sending his own Son in the likeness of sinful flesh,</u> and for sin, condemned sin in the flesh:*

> *Philippians 2:7*
> *But made himself of no reputation, and took upon him the form of a servant, <u>and was made in the likeness of men:</u>*

> *John 1:14*
> <u>*And the Word was made flesh,*</u> *and dwelt among us, <u>(and we beheld his glory, the glory as of the only begotten of the Father,)</u> full of grace and truth.*

> *1Chronicles 17:11 - 14*
> *11 - <u>And it shall come to pass, when thy days be expired that thou must go to be with thy fathers, that I will raise up thy seed after thee, which shall be of thy sons; and I will establish his kingdom.</u>*
> *12 - <u>He shall build me an house, and I will stablish his throne for ever.</u>*
> *13 - <u>I will be his father, and he shall be my son: and I will not take my mercy away from him, as I took it from him that was before thee:</u>*
> *14 - <u>But I will settle him in mine house and in my kingdom for ever: and his throne shall be established for evermore.</u>*

> *Romans 1:3*
> <u>*Concerning his Son Jesus Christ our Lord, which was made of the seed of David according to the flesh;*</u>

His seed would bring forth an everlasting kingdom that shall not end. Mercy shall never be taken away from him. The covenant made with Noah was made without condition by an oath.

> *Isaiah 54:7 – 10*
> *7 - For a small moment have I forsaken thee; but with great mercies will I gather thee.*
> *8 - <u>In a little wrath I hid my face from thee for a moment; but with everlasting kindness will I have mercy on thee, saith the LORD thy Redeemer.</u>*
> *9 - <u>For this is as the waters of Noah unto me: for as I have sworn that the waters of Noah should no more go over the earth; so have I sworn that I would not be wroth with thee, nor rebuke thee.</u>*
> *10 - For the mountains shall depart, and the hills be removed; but my kindness shall not depart from thee, <u>neither shall the covenant of my peace be removed</u>, saith the LORD that hath mercy on thee.*

Acts 13:21 – 23
21 - And afterward they desired a king: and God gave unto them Saul the son of Cis, a man of the tribe of Benjamin, by the space of forty years.
22 - And when he had removed him, he raised up unto them David to be their king; to whom also he gave testimony, and said, <u>I have found David the son of Jesse, a man after mine own heart, which shall fulfil all my will.</u>
23 - <u>Of this man's seed hath God according to his promise raised unto Israel a Saviour, Jesus:</u>

Hebrews 7:19 – 21
19 - For the law made nothing perfect, but the bringing in of a better hope did; by the which we draw nigh unto God.
20 - <u>And inasmuch as not without an oath he was made priest:</u>
21 - <u>(For those priests were made without an oath; but this with an oath by him that said unto him, The Lord sware and will not repent, Thou art a priest for ever after the order of Melchisedec:)</u>

Adam was sent forth out of the garden, but the seed of David would remain in the presence of God forever.

1Chronicles 17:13 – 14
13 - <u>I will be his father, and he shall be my son: and I will not take my mercy away from him, as I took it from him that was before thee:</u>
14 - <u>But I will settle him in mine house and in my kingdom for ever: and his throne shall be established for evermore.</u>

2Timothy 2:8
Remember that <u>Jesus Christ of the seed of David was raised from the dead</u> according to my gospel:

THE SEED OF DAVID AND THE SON OF GOD

Revelation 22:16
I Jesus have sent mine angel to testify unto you these things in the churches. <u>I am the root and the offspring of David,</u> and the bright and morning star.

Matthew 3:17
And lo a voice from heaven, saying, This is my beloved Son, in whom I am well pleased.

Matthew 17:5
While he yet spake, behold, a bright cloud overshadowed them: and behold a voice out of the cloud, which said, This is my beloved Son, in whom I am well pleased; hear ye him

Luke 3:22
And the Holy Ghost descended in a bodily shape like a dove upon him, and a voice came from heaven, which said, Thou art my beloved Son; in thee I am well pleased.

> *2Peter 1:17*
> *For he received from God the Father honour and glory, when there came such a voice to him from the excellent glory, This is my beloved Son, in whom I am well pleased.*

APPOINTED

David was appointed to be king to replace Saul who the LORD rejected. Seth means appointed.

> *1Samuel 15:28*
> *And Samuel said unto him, The LORD hath rent the kingdom of Israel from thee this day, <u>and hath given it to a neighbour of thine, that is better than thou.</u>*

> *1Samuel 16:1, 13 – 14*
> *1 - And the LORD said unto Samuel, How long wilt thou mourn for Saul, seeing I have rejected him from reigning over Israel? fill thine horn with oil, and go, I will send thee to Jesse the Bethlehemite: <u>for I have provided me a king among his sons.</u>*
>
> *13 - <u>Then Samuel took the horn of oil, and anointed him in the midst of his brethren: and the Spirit of the LORD came upon David from that day forward.</u> So Samuel rose up, and went to Ramah.*
> *14 - <u>But the Spirit of the LORD departed from Saul, and an evil spirit from the LORD troubled him.</u>*

> *Acts 13:21 – 23*
> *21 - And afterward they desired a king: and God gave unto them Saul the son of Cis, a man of the tribe of Benjamin, by the space of forty years.*
> *22 - <u>And when he had removed him, he raised up unto them David to be their king; to whom also he gave testimony, and said, I have found David the son of Jesse, a man after mine own heart, which shall fulfil all my will.</u>*
> *23 - <u>Of this man's seed hath God according to his promise raised unto Israel a Saviour, Jesus:</u>*

Saul was a type of the covenant of law that would be replaced by a covenant of faith. His kingship was subject to the law and the Levitical priesthood. He could not operate as a kingly priest. When he gave the burnt offering, he disobeyed the commandment of the LORD God.

> *Leviticus 1:3, 7 – 8, 13*
> *3 - <u>If his offering be a burnt sacrifice of the herd</u>, let him offer a male without blemish: he shall offer it of his own voluntary will <u>at the door of the tabernacle of the congregation before the LORD.</u>*

7 - And the sons of Aaron the priest shall put fire upon the altar, and lay the wood in order upon the fire:
8 - And the priests, Aaron's sons, shall lay the parts, the head, and the fat, in order upon the wood that is on the fire which is upon the altar:

13 - But he shall wash the inwards and the legs with water: and the priest shall bring it all, and burn it upon the altar: it is a burnt sacrifice, an offering made by fire, of a sweet savour unto the LORD.

1Samuel 13:8 – 14
8 - And he tarried seven days, according to the set time that Samuel had appointed: but Samuel came not to Gilgal; and the people were scattered from him.
9 - And Saul said, Bring hither a burnt offering to me, and peace offerings. And he offered the burnt offering.
10 - And it came to pass, that as soon as he had made an end of offering the burnt offering, behold, Samuel came; and Saul went out to meet him, that he might salute him.
11 - And Samuel said, What hast thou done? And Saul said, Because I saw that the people were scattered from me, and that thou camest not within the days appointed, and that the Philistines gathered themselves together at Michmash;
12 - Therefore said I, The Philistines will come down now upon me to Gilgal, and I have not made supplication unto the LORD: I forced myself therefore, and offered a burnt offering.
13 - And Samuel said to Saul, Thou hast done foolishly: thou hast not kept the commandment of the LORD thy God, which he commanded thee: for now would the LORD have established thy kingdom upon Israel for ever.
14 - But now thy kingdom shall not continue: the LORD hath sought him a man after his own heart, and the LORD hath commanded him to be captain over his people, because thou hast not kept that which the LORD commanded thee.

Because of Saul offering the burnt sacrifice himself the LORD gave his kingdom to another, the LORD sought him a man after his own heart to be king instead of Saul. Abraham offered burnt sacrifice, Jethro offered burnt sacrifice and Moses when consecrating Aaron and his sons. This was done in faith but when the law came, only the priests could offer burnt sacrifice.

Genesis 22:13
And Abraham lifted up his eyes, and looked, and behold behind him a ram caught in a thicket by his horns: and Abraham went and took the ram, and offered him up for a burnt offering in the stead of his son.

Exodus 18:12
And Jethro, Moses' father in law, took a burnt offering and sacrifices for God: and Aaron came, and all the elders of Israel, to eat bread with Moses' father in law before God.

> *Exodus 28:1*
> *And take thou unto thee Aaron thy brother, and his sons with him, from among the children of Israel, that he may minister unto me in the priest's office, even Aaron, Nadab and Abihu, Eleazar and Ithamar, Aaron's sons.*
>
> *Exodus 29:18*
> *And thou shalt burn the whole ram upon the altar: it is a burnt offering unto the LORD: it is <u>a sweet savour, an offering made by fire unto the LORD</u>.*

Because of Saul disobeying the commandment he lost the kingdom. Under the law if you did not obey one point you disobeyed the whole law.

> *James 2:10*
> *For whosoever shall keep the whole law, <u>and yet offend in one point, he is guilty of all</u>.*
>
> *Galatians 3:10*
> *For as many as are of the works of the law are under the curse: for it is written, <u>Cursed is every one that continueth not in all things which are written in the book of the law to do them</u>.*

David was a type of the covenant of faith. He operated as both king and priest. He was not subject to the Levitical law.

> *2Samuel 6:12 – 19*
> *12 - And it was told king David, saying, The LORD hath blessed the house of Obededom, and all that pertaineth unto him, because of the ark of God. <u>So David went and brought up the ark of God from the house of Obededom into the city of David with gladness.</u>*
> *13 - And it was so, that when they that bare the ark of the LORD had gone six paces, <u>he sacrificed oxen and fatlings.</u>*
> *14 - <u>And David danced before the LORD with all his might; and David was girded with a linen ephod.</u>*
> *15 - So David and all the house of Israel brought up the ark of the LORD with shouting, and with the sound of the trumpet.*
> *16 - And as the ark of the LORD came into the city of David, Michal Saul's daughter looked through a window, and saw king David leaping and dancing before the LORD; and she despised him in her heart.*
> *17 - And they brought in the ark of the LORD, and set it in his place, in the midst of the tabernacle that David had pitched for it: <u>and David offered burnt offerings and peace offerings before the LORD.</u>*
> *18 - <u>And as soon as David had made an end of offering burnt offerings and peace offerings, he blessed the people in the name of the LORD of hosts.</u>*
> *19 - <u>And he dealt among all the people, even among the whole multitude of Israel, as well to the women as men, to every one a cake of bread, and a good piece of flesh, and a flagon of wine. So all the people departed every one to his house.</u>*

David offered the sacrifice, oxen and fatlings dressed in a linen ephod. He offered the Burnt offerings and the peace offerings before the LORD. He blessed the people and gave them bread, flesh and wine. He gave to the women as well as to the men.

Under the Levitical Priesthood:
- Only Aaron's sons could offer to the LORD. David was of Judah.
- Women were excluded. In the Levitical priesthood only
- The priests could bless the people.
- Only the priests could wear the linen ephod.

Leviticus 1:7 – 8
7 - *And the sons of Aaron the priest shall put fire upon the altar, and lay the wood in order upon the fire:*
8 - *And the priests, Aaron's sons, shall lay the parts, the head, and the fat, in order upon the wood that is on the fire which is upon the altar:*

Deuteronomy 21:5
And the priests the sons of Levi shall come near; for them the LORD thy God hath chosen to minister unto him, and to bless in the name of the LORD; and by their word shall every controversy and every stroke be tried:

Numbers 6:22 – 27
22 - And the LORD spake unto Moses, saying,
3 - *Speak unto Aaron and unto his sons, saying, On this wise ye shall bless the children of Israel, saying unto them,*
24 - The LORD bless thee, and keep thee:
25 - The LORD make his face shine upon thee, and be gracious unto thee:
26 - The LORD lift up his countenance upon thee, and give thee peace.
27 - And they shall put my name upon the children of Israel; and I will bless them.

1Samuel 2:18
But Samuel ministered before the LORD, being a child, *girded with a linen ephod.*

1Samuel 22:17 - 18
17 - And the king said unto the footmen that stood about him, *Turn, and slay the priests of the LORD;* because their hand also is with David, and because they knew when he fled, and did not shew it to me. But the servants of the king would not put forth their hand to fall upon the priests of the LORD.
18 - And the king said to Doeg, Turn thou, and fall upon the priests. And Doeg the Edomite turned*, and he fell upon the priests, and slew on that day fourscore and five persons that did wear a linen ephod.*

The new covenant would be given to both men and women. Just as David gave to both men and women. Under the new covenant we would all be one.

2Samuel 6:19
And he dealt among all the people, even among the whole multitude of Israel, as well to the <u>women as men, to every one a cake of bread, and a good piece of flesh, and a flagon of wine. So all the people departed every one to his house.</u>

Joel 2:28 – 29
28 - And it shall come to pass afterward, that I will pour out my spirit upon all flesh; <u>and your sons and your daughters shall prophesy,</u> your old men shall dream dreams, your young men shall see visions:
29 - And also upon <u>the servants and upon the handmaids</u> in those days will I pour out my spirit.

Acts 5:14
And believers were the more added to the Lord, multitudes both of <u>men and women.</u>)

Acts 8:12
But when they believed Philip preaching the things concerning the kingdom of God, and the name of Jesus Christ, they were baptized, <u>both men and women.</u>

Galatians 3:24 – 29
24 - Wherefore the law was our schoolmaster to bring us unto Christ, that we might be justified by faith.
25 - But after that faith is come, we are no longer under a schoolmaster.
26 - For ye are all the children of God by faith in Christ Jesus.
27 - For as many of you as have been baptized into Christ have put on Christ.
28 - There is neither Jew nor Greek, there is neither bond nor free, <u>there is neither male nor female: for ye are all one in Christ Jesus.</u>
29 - And if ye be Christ's, then are ye Abraham's seed, and heirs according to the promise.

The LORD made an everlasting covenant with David, that his seed would become a royal priesthood.

1Chronicles 17:10 – 14
10 - And since the time that I commanded judges to be over my people Israel. Moreover I will subdue all thine enemies. <u>Furthermore I tell thee that the LORD will build thee an house.</u>
11 - <u>And it shall come to pass, when thy days be expired that thou must go to be with thy fathers, that I will raise up thy seed after thee, which shall be of thy sons; and I will establish his kingdom.</u>
12 - <u>He shall build me an house, and I will stablish his throne for ever.</u>
13 - <u>I will be his father, and he shall be my son: and I will not take my mercy away from</u> him, as I took it from him that was before thee:

14 - But I will settle him in mine house and in my kingdom for ever: and his throne shall be established for evermore.

2Chronicles 21:7
Howbeit the LORD would not destroy the house of David, <u>because of the covenant that he had made with David, and as he promised to give a light to him and to his sons for ever.</u>

John 7:42
Hath not the scripture said, <u>That Christ cometh of the seed of David,</u> and out of the town of Bethlehem, where David was?

Hebrews 7:13 – 14
13 - For he of whom these things are spoken pertaineth to another tribe, of which no man gave attendance at the altar.
14 - <u>For it is evident that our Lord sprang out of Juda;</u> of which tribe Moses spake nothing concerning priesthood.

Hebrews 7:11 – 25
11 - If therefore perfection were by the Levitical priesthood, (for under it the people received the law,) what further need was there that another priest should rise after the order of Melchisedec, and not be called after the order of Aaron?
12 - <u>For the priesthood being changed, there is made of necessity a change also of the law.</u>
13 - For he of whom these things are spoken pertaineth to another tribe, of which no man gave attendance at the altar.
14 - <u>For it is evident that our Lord sprang out of Juda;</u> of which tribe Moses spake nothing concerning priesthood.
15 - <u>And it is yet far more evident: for that after the similitude of Melchisedec there ariseth another priest,</u>
16 - <u>Who is made, not after the law of a carnal commandment, but after the power of an endless life.</u>
17 - <u>For he testifieth, Thou art a priest for ever after the order of Melchisedec.</u>
18 - For there is verily a disannulling of the commandment going before for the weakness and unprofitableness thereof.
19 - For the law made nothing perfect, but the bringing in of a better hope did; by the which we draw nigh unto God.
20 - And inasmuch as not without an oath he was made priest:
21 - (For those priests were made without an oath; but this with an oath by him that said unto him, The Lord sware and will not repent, Thou art a priest for ever after the order of Melchisedec:)
22 - <u>By so much was Jesus made a surety of a better testament.</u>
23 - And they truly were many priests, because they were not suffered to continue by reason of death:
24 - <u>But this man, because he continueth ever, hath an unchangeable priesthood.</u>
25 - <u>Wherefore he is able also to save them to the uttermost that come unto God by him, seeing he ever liveth to make intercession for them.</u>

1Peter 2:9
But ye are a chosen generation, a royal priesthood, an holy nation, a peculiar people; that ye should shew forth the praises of him who hath called you out of darkness into his marvellous light:

When David brought the Ark of the Covenant back to Jerusalem it was a symbol of the ushering in of a new and better covenant. The LORD promised to rebuild the tabernacle of David that would include all flesh. David's tabernacle was built on Mount Moriah where Abraham offered up Isaac, and Solomon, David's son built the temple. The mountain of faith where God provided the ram for Abraham and stayed the plague for David.

Genesis 22:1 – 2, 7 – 8, 10 - 14
1 - And it came to pass after these things, that God did tempt Abraham, and said unto him, Abraham: and he said, Behold, here I am.
2 - And he said, Take now thy son, thine only son Isaac, whom thou lovest, and get thee into the land of Moriah; and offer him there for a burnt offering upon one of the mountains which I will tell thee of.

7 - And Isaac spake unto Abraham his father, and said, My father: and he said, Here am I, my son. And he said, Behold the fire and the wood: but where is the lamb for a burnt offering?
8 - And Abraham said, My son, God will provide himself a lamb for a burnt offering: so they went both of them together.

10 - And Abraham stretched forth his hand, and took the knife to slay his son.
11 - And the angel of the LORD called unto him out of heaven, and said, Abraham, Abraham: and he said, Here am I.
12 - And he said, Lay not thine hand upon the lad, neither do thou any thing unto him: for now I know that thou fearest God, seeing thou hast not withheld thy son, thine only son from me.
13 - And Abraham lifted up his eyes, and looked, and behold behind him a ram caught in a thicket by his horns: and Abraham went and took the ram, and offered him up for a burnt offering in the stead of his son.
14 - And Abraham called the name of that place Jehovahjireh: as it is said to this day, In the mount of the LORD it shall be seen.

1Chronicles 21:22, 26 – 30
22 - Then David said to Ornan, Grant me the place of this threshingfloor, that I may build an altar therein unto the LORD: thou shalt grant it me for the full price: that the plague may be stayed from the people.

26 - And David built there an altar unto the LORD, and offered burnt offerings and peace offerings, and called upon the LORD; and he answered him from heaven by fire upon the altar of burnt offering.
27 - And the LORD commanded the angel; and he put up his sword again into the sheath thereof.
28 - At that time when David saw that the LORD had answered him in the threshingfloor of Ornan the Jebusite, then he sacrificed there.

29 - <u>For the tabernacle of the LORD, which Moses made in the wilderness, and the altar of the burnt offering, were at that season in the high place at Gibeon.</u>
30 - <u>But David could not go before it to enquire of God: for he was afraid because of the sword of the angel of the LORD.</u>

2Chronicles 3:1
<u>Then Solomon began to build the house of the LORD at Jerusalem in mount Moriah, where the LORD appeared unto David his father, in the place that David had prepared in the threshingfloor of Ornan the Jebusite.</u>

David could not go to the tabernacle of Moses because of the sword of the angel of the LORD. This represents a changing of the covenant. David's kingdom would be a kingdom of kings and priests, a royal priesthood.

Revelation 1:5 – 6
5 - And from Jesus Christ, who is the faithful witness, and the first begotten of the dead, and the prince of the kings of the earth. Unto him that loved us, and washed us from our sins in his own blood,
6 - <u>And hath made us kings and priests unto God and his Father</u>; to him be glory and dominion for ever and ever. Amen.

Revelation 5:6 – 10
6 - And I beheld, and, lo, in the midst of the throne and of the four beasts, and in the midst of the elders, stood a Lamb as it had been slain, having seven horns and seven eyes, which are the seven Spirits of God sent forth into all the earth.
7 - And he came and took the book out of the right hand of him that sat upon the throne.
8 - And when he had taken the book, the four beasts and four and twenty elders fell down before the Lamb, having every one of them harps, and golden vials full of odours, which are the prayers of saints.
9 - And they sung a new song, saying, Thou art worthy to take the book, and to open the seals thereof: for thou wast slain, and hast redeemed us to God by thy blood out of every kindred, and tongue, and people, and nation;
10 - <u>And hast made us unto our God kings and priests: and we shall reign on the earth.</u>

Acts 7:44 – 46
44 - Our fathers had the tabernacle of witness in the wilderness, as he had appointed, speaking unto Moses, that he should make it according to the fashion that he had seen.
45 - <u>Which also our fathers that came after brought in with Jesus into the possession of the Gentiles, whom God drave out before the face of our fathers, unto the days of David;</u>
46 - <u>Who found favour before God, and desired to find a tabernacle for the God of Jacob.</u>

Acts 15:14 – 17
14 - Simeon hath declared how God at the first did visit the Gentiles, to take out of them a people for his name.
15 - And to this agree the words of the prophets; as it is written,
16 - <u>After this I will return, and will build again the tabernacle of David, which is fallen down; and I will build again the ruins thereof, and I will set it up:</u>
17 - <u>That the residue of men might seek after the Lord, and all the Gentiles, upon whom my name is called, saith the Lord, who doeth all these things.</u>

Galatians 3:28
There is neither Jew nor Greek, there is neither bond nor free, there is neither male nor female: for ye are all one in Christ Jesus.

Saul would be replaced by David, the same as Abel would be replaced by Seth. He is another seed who would have a son so that men would call upon the name of the LORD, the God of covenant, the redeemer of Israel. John was born to be a forerunner to the Christ, the Son of David.

Luke 1:66 – 80
66 - And all they that heard them laid them up in their hearts, saying, What manner of child shall this be! And the hand of the Lord was with him.
67 - And his father Zacharias was filled with the Holy Ghost, and prophesied, saying,
68 - Blessed be the Lord God of Israel; for he hath visited and redeemed his people,
69 - And hath raised up an horn of salvation for us in the house of his servant David;
70 - As he spake by the mouth of his holy prophets, which have been since the world began:
71 - That we should be saved from our enemies, and from the hand of all that hate us;
72 - To perform the mercy promised to our fathers, and to remember his holy covenant;
73 - The oath which he sware to our father Abraham,
74 - That he would grant unto us, that we being delivered out of the hand of our enemies might serve him without fear,
75 - In holiness and righteousness before him, all the days of our life.
76 - <u>And thou, child, shalt be called the prophet of the Highest: for thou shalt go before the face of the Lord to prepare his ways;</u>
77 - <u>To give knowledge of salvation unto his people by the remission of their sins,</u>
78 - Through the tender mercy of our God; whereby the dayspring from on high hath visited us,
79 - To give light to them that sit in darkness and in the shadow of death, to guide our feet into the way of peace.
80 - And the child grew, and waxed strong in spirit, and was in the deserts till the day of his shewing unto Israel.

Galatians 3:13 – 14
13 - Christ hath redeemed us from the curse of the law, being made a curse for us: for it is written, Cursed is every one that hangeth on a tree:
14 - That the blessing of Abraham might come on the Gentiles through Jesus Christ; that we might receive the promise of the Spirit through faith.

David was a type of the redeemed. He was an adulterer and a murderer just as the children of the kingdom that the Son of God came to save.

Isaiah 1:18
Come now, and let us reason together, saith the LORD: <u>though your sins be as scarlet, they shall be as white as snow; though they be red like crimson, they shall be as wool.</u>

2Samuel 12:1 – 13
1 - And the LORD sent Nathan unto David. And he came unto him, and said unto him, There were two men in one city; the one rich, and the other poor.
2 - The rich man had exceeding many flocks and herds:
3 - But the poor man had nothing, save one little ewe lamb, which he had bought and nourished up: and it grew up together with him, and with his children; it did eat of his own meat, and drank of his own cup, and lay in his bosom, and was unto him as a daughter.
4 - And there came a traveller unto the rich man, and he spared to take of his own flock and of his own herd, to dress for the wayfaring man that was come unto him; but took the poor man's lamb, and dressed it for the man that was come to him.
5 - And David's anger was greatly kindled against the man; and he said to Nathan, As the LORD liveth, <u>the man that hath done this thing shall surely die:</u>
6 - And he shall restore the lamb fourfold, because he did this thing, and because he had no pity.
7 - And Nathan said to David, <u>Thou art the man</u>. Thus saith the LORD God of Israel, I anointed thee king over Israel, and I delivered thee out of the hand of Saul;
8 - And I gave thee thy master's house, and thy master's wives into thy bosom, and gave thee the house of Israel and of Judah; and if that had been too little, I would moreover have given unto thee such and such things.
9 - <u>Wherefore hast thou despised the commandment of the LORD, to do evil in his sight? thou hast killed Uriah the Hittite with the sword, and hast taken his wife to be thy wife, and hast slain him with the sword of the children of Ammon.</u>
10 - Now therefore the sword shall never depart from thine house; because thou hast despised me, and hast taken the wife of Uriah the Hittite to be thy wife.
11 - Thus saith the LORD, Behold, I will raise up evil against thee out of thine own house, and I will take thy wives before thine eyes, and give them unto thy neighbour, and he shall lie with thy wives in the sight of this sun.
12 - For thou didst it secretly: but I will do this thing before all Israel, and before the sun.

13 - <u>And David said unto Nathan, I have sinned against the LORD. And Nathan said unto David, The LORD also hath put away thy sin; thou shalt not die.</u>

Mark 8:38
Whosoever therefore shall be ashamed of me and of my words in this <u>adulterous and sinful generation</u>; of him also shall the Son of man be ashamed, when he cometh in the glory of his Father with the holy angels.

John 8:41 – 44
41 - Ye do the deeds of your father. Then said they to him, We be not born of fornication; we have one Father, even God.
42 - Jesus said unto them, If God were your Father, ye would love me: for I proceeded forth and came from God; neither came I of myself, but he sent me.
43 - Why do ye not understand my speech? even because ye cannot hear my word.
44 - <u>Ye are of your father the devil, and the lusts of your father ye will do. He was a murderer from the beginning, and abode not in the truth,</u> because there is no truth in him. When he speaketh a lie, he speaketh of his own: for he is a liar, and the father of it.

1Timothy 1:9 – 10
9 - Knowing this, <u>that the law is not made for a righteous man, but for the lawless and disobedient, for the ungodly and for sinners, for unholy and profane, for murderers of fathers and murderers of mothers, for manslayers,</u>
10 - <u>For whoremongers, for them that defile themselves with mankind, for menstealers, for liars, for perjured persons, and if there be any other thing that is contrary to sound doctrine;</u>

The law was given to show how exceeding sinful we are. David was confronted by the prophet Nathan about his sin. He told a story of a lamb who was taken and slaughtered for a traveler. The poor man's only lamb. David was angry and pronounced death upon the man who did this, but Nathan replied you are that man. When David confessed Nathan told him that his sin had been removed. This is comparable of the lamb that was slain to take away the sins of the world.

2Samuel 12:1 – 4, 13
1 - And the LORD sent Nathan unto David. And he came unto him, and said unto him, There were two men in one city; the one rich, and the other poor.
2 - The rich man had exceeding many flocks and herds:
3 - But the poor man had nothing, save one little ewe lamb, which he had bought and nourished up: and it grew up together with him, and with his children; it did eat of his own meat, and drank of his own cup, and lay in his bosom, and was unto him as a daughter.
4 - And there came a traveller unto the rich man, and he spared to take of his own flock and of his own herd, to dress for the wayfaring man that was come unto him; but took the poor man's lamb, and dressed it for the man that was come to him.

13 - And David said unto Nathan, I have sinned against the LORD. And Nathan said unto David, The LORD also hath put away thy sin; thou shalt not die.

Zechariah 12:10
And I will pour upon the house of David, and upon the inhabitants of Jerusalem, the spirit of grace and of supplications: and they shall look upon me whom they have pierced, and they shall mourn for him, as one mourneth for his only son, and shall be in bitterness for him, as one that is in bitterness for his firstborn.

John 3:16 – 18
16 - For God so loved the world, that he gave his only begotten Son, that whosoever believeth in him should not perish, but have everlasting life.
17 - For God sent not his Son into the world to condemn the world; but that the world through him might be saved.
18 - He that believeth on him is not condemned: but he that believeth not is condemned already, because he hath not believed in the name of the only begotten Son of God.

John 1:29
The next day John seeth Jesus coming unto him, and saith, Behold the Lamb of God, which taketh away the sin of the world.

John 1:36
And looking upon Jesus as he walked, he saith, Behold the Lamb of God!

John stated that condemnation would come to those who did not believe in the name of the only begotten Son of God. We read that Seth had a son and he called his name Enos and men began to call on the name of the LORD. We know that LORD refers to covenant God. Thus, the son of Seth would bring to men the name of the covenant God.

Genesis 4:26
And to Seth, to him also there was born a son; and he called his name Enos: then began men to call upon the name of the LORD.

The children of Israel would know him by another name, (Jehovah) Abraham, Isaac and Jacob did not know. We know that the covenant given to Abraham was by faith, this name that Abraham did not know was under the covenant of Law. But God would give to them a new name. It would come through the house of David.

Exodus 6:2 – 4
2 - And God spake unto Moses, and said unto him, I am the LORD:
3 - And I appeared unto Abraham, unto Isaac, and unto Jacob, by the name of God Almighty, but by my name JEHOVAH was I not known to them.
4 - And I have also established my covenant with them, to give them the land of Canaan, the land of their pilgrimage, wherein they were strangers.

Isaiah 62:1 - 2
1 - <u>For Zion's sake will I not hold my peace, and for Jerusalem's sake I will not rest, until the righteousness thereof go forth as brightness, and the salvation thereof as a lamp that burneth.</u>
2 - <u>And the Gentiles shall see thy righteousness, and all kings thy glory: and thou shalt be called by a new name, which the mouth of the LORD shall name.</u>

Zechariah 13:1, 9
1 - <u>In that day there shall be a fountain opened to the house of David and to the inhabitants of Jerusalem for sin and for uncleanness.</u>

9 - And I will bring the third part through the fire, and will refine them as silver is refined, and will try them as gold is tried: <u>they shall call on my name, and I will hear them: I will say, It is my people: and they shall say, The LORD is my God.</u>

Zechariah 14:9
<u>And the LORD shall be king over all the earth: in that day shall there be one LORD, and his name one.</u>

Matthew 1:21
And she shall bring forth a son, <u>and thou shalt call his name JESUS: for he shall save his people from their sins.</u>

Matthew 12:21
And in his name shall the Gentiles trust.

John 5:43
<u>I am come in my Father's name</u>, and ye receive me not: if another shall come in his own name, him ye will receive.

John 12:28
Father, glorify thy name. Then came there a voice from heaven, saying, I have both glorified it, and will glorify it again.

John 14:26
<u>But the Comforter, which is the Holy Ghost, whom the Father will send in my name,</u> he shall teach you all things, and bring all things to your remembrance, whatsoever I have said unto you.

John 17:6
<u>I have manifested thy name</u> unto the men which thou gavest me out of the world: thine they were, and thou gavest them me; and they have kept thy word.

John 17:11 - 12
11 - And now I am no more in the world, but these are in the world, and I come to thee. Holy Father, <u>keep through thine own name those whom thou hast given me, that they may be one, as we are.</u>

12 - While I was with them in the world, <u>I kept them in thy name</u>: those that thou gavest me I have kept, and none of them is lost, but the son of perdition; that the scripture might be fulfilled.

John 17:26
<u>*And I have declared unto them thy name, and will declare it:*</u> *that the love wherewith thou hast loved me may be in them, and I in them.*

John 20:31
But these are written, that ye might believe that Jesus is the Christ, the Son of God; <u>*and that believing ye might have life through his name.*</u>

MEN BEGAN TO CALL ON THE NAME OF THE LORD

<u>For salvation</u>

Acts 2:21
And it shall come to pass, <u>*that whosoever shall call on the name of the Lord shall be saved.*</u>

Acts 2:38
Then Peter said unto them, Repent, <u>*and be baptized every one of you in the name of Jesus Christ for the remission of sins,*</u> *and ye shall receive the gift of the Holy Ghost.*

Acts 4:12
<u>*Neither is there salvation in any other: for there is none other name under heaven given among men, whereby we must be saved.*</u>

Romans 10:13
<u>*For whosoever shall call upon the name of the Lord shall be saved.*</u>

<u>For healing, signs and wonders</u>

Acts 3:16
<u>*And his name through faith in his name hath made this man strong,*</u> *whom ye see and know: yea, the faith which is by him hath given him this perfect soundness in the presence of you all.*

Acts 4:30
By stretching forth thine hand to heal; <u>*and that signs and wonders may be done by the name of thy holy child Jesus.*</u>

In Baptism

Acts 2:38
Then Peter said unto them, Repent, <u>and be baptized every one of you in the name of Jesus Christ for the remission of sins,</u> and ye shall receive the gift of the Holy Ghost.

Acts 8:12
But when they believed Philip preaching the things concerning the kingdom of God<u>, and the name of Jesus Christ, they were baptized, both men and women.</u>

Acts 8:14 – 16
14 - Now when the apostles which were at Jerusalem heard that Samaria had received the word of God, they sent unto them Peter and John:
15 - Who, when they were come down, prayed for them, that they might receive the Holy Ghost:
16 - (For as yet he was fallen upon none of them: <u>only they were baptized in the name of the Lord Jesus.</u>)

Acts 10:45 – 48
45 - And they of the circumcision which believed were astonished, as many as came with Peter, because that on the Gentiles also was poured out the gift of the Holy Ghost.
46 - For they heard them speak with tongues, and magnify God. Then answered Peter,
47 - Can any man forbid water, that these should not be baptized, which have received the Holy Ghost as well as we?
48 - <u>And he commanded them to be baptized in the name of the Lord</u>. Then prayed they him to tarry certain days.

Acts 19:1 – 6
1 - And it came to pass, that, while Apollos was at Corinth, Paul having passed through the upper coasts came to Ephesus: and finding certain disciples,
2 - He said unto them, Have ye received the Holy Ghost since ye believed? And they said unto him, We have not so much as heard whether there be any Holy Ghost.
3 - And he said unto them, Unto what then were ye baptized? And they said, Unto John's baptism.
4 - <u>Then said Paul, John verily baptized with the baptism of repentance, saying unto the people, that they should believe on him which should come after him, that is, on Christ Jesus.</u>
5 - <u>When they heard this, they were baptized in the name of the Lord Jesus.</u>
6 - And when Paul had laid his hands upon them, the Holy Ghost came on them; and they spake with tongues, and prophesied.

In all things

Philippians 2:9 – 10
9 - Wherefore God also hath highly exalted him, and given him a name which is above every name:
10 - That at the name of Jesus every knee should bow, of things in heaven, and things in earth, and things under the earth;

Colossians 3:17
And whatsoever ye do in word or deed, do all in the name of the Lord Jesus, giving thanks to God and the Father by him.

1John 3:23
And this is his commandment, That we should believe on the name of his Son Jesus Christ, and love one another, as he gave us commandment.

1John 5:13
These things have I written unto you that believe on the name of the Son of God; that ye may know that ye have eternal life, and that ye may believe on the name of the Son of God.

Revelation 22:4
And they shall see his face; and his name shall be in their foreheads.

PARADISE, THE PLACE OF COVENANT.

This final covenant brings salvation and eternal life to a fallen world. Reconciliation of lost sons to a loving father.

> *2Corinthians 5:19*
> *To wit, that God was in Christ, reconciling the world unto himself, not imputing their trespasses unto them; and hath committed unto us the word of reconciliation.*

When Jesus was on the cross he made a promise to the thief that he would be with him in Paradise that day. The promise was fulfilled because the old was replaced with the new at the death of the testator. Paradise was the place of the covenant. Jesus was saying to the thief that the covenant of faith would be established at the time of his death. All who believed would now have access to the Paradise of The LORD God.

> *Luke 23:42 – 43*
> *42 - And he said unto Jesus, Lord, remember me when thou comest into thy kingdom.*
> *43 - And Jesus said unto him, Verily I say unto thee, <u>To day shalt thou be with me in paradise.</u>*

> *Hebrews 9:15 - 17*
> *15 - <u>And for this cause he is the mediator of the new testament, that by means of death, for the redemption of the transgressions that were under the first testament, they which are called might receive the promise of eternal inheritance.</u>*
> *16 - <u>For where a testament is, there must also of necessity be the death of the testator.</u>*
> *17 - <u>For a testament is of force after men are dead: otherwise it is of no strength at all while the testator liveth.</u>*

I will end this study with Paul's letter to the Ephesians and I pray that you will continue to seek revelation knowledge of the One who loves you.

Ephesians 3:1 – 21
1 - For this cause I Paul, the prisoner of Jesus Christ for you Gentiles,
2 - If ye have heard of the dispensation of the grace of God which is given me to you-ward:
3 - How that by revelation he made known unto me the mystery; (as I wrote afore in few words,
4 - Whereby, when ye read, ye may understand my knowledge in the mystery of Christ)
5 - Which in other ages was not made known unto the sons of men, as it is now revealed unto his holy apostles and prophets by the Spirit;
6 - That the Gentiles should be fellowheirs, and of the same body, and partakers of his promise in Christ by the gospel:
7 - Whereof I was made a minister, according to the gift of the grace of God given unto me by the effectual working of his power.
8 - Unto me, who am less than the least of all saints, is this grace given, that I should preach among the Gentiles the unsearchable riches of Christ;
9 - And to make all men see what is the fellowship of the mystery, which from the beginning of the world hath been hid in God, who created all things by Jesus Christ:
10 - To the intent that now unto the principalities and powers in heavenly places might be known by the church the manifold wisdom of God,
11 - According to the eternal purpose which he purposed in Christ Jesus our Lord:
12 - In whom we have boldness and access with confidence by the faith of him.
13 - Wherefore I desire that ye faint not at my tribulations for you, which is your glory.
14 - For this cause I bow my knees unto the Father of our Lord Jesus Christ,
16 - That he would grant you, according to the riches of his glory, to be strengthened with might by his Spirit in the inner man;
17 - That Christ may dwell in your hearts by faith; that ye, being rooted and grounded in love,
18 - May be able to comprehend with all saints what is the breadth, and length, and depth, and height;
19 - And to know the love of Christ, which passeth knowledge, that ye might be filled with all the fulness of God.
20 - Now unto him that is able to do exceeding abundantly above all that we ask or think, according to the power that worketh in us,
21 - Unto him be glory in the church by Christ Jesus throughout all ages, world without end. Amen.

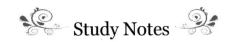

Made in the USA
Lexington, KY
07 October 2018